ROASTS, BRAISES & GRILLS

ROASTS, BRAISES & GRILLS

Consulting Editor

Linda Fraser

HERMES HOUSE

First published in 1999 by Hermes House

Hermes House books are available for bulk purchase for sales promotion and
premium use. For details, write or call the sales director,
Hermes House, 27 West 20th Street, New York, NY 10011;
(800) 354-9657

© Anness Publishing Limited 1998

Hermes House is an imprint of
Anness Publishing Inc.

ISBN 1-84038-206-6

Publisher: Joanna Lorenz
Senior Cookbook Editor: Linda Fraser
Introduction: Jenni Fleetwood
Designer: Brian Weldon
Indexer: Hilary Bird
Photography: Karl Adamson, Edward Allwright, Steve Baxter, James Duncan,
Michelle Garrett, Amanda Heywood, William Lingwood, David Jordan,
Patrick McLeavey and Tom Odulate
Food for Photography: Jacqueline Clark, Joanna Farrow, Nicola Fowler, Shirley
Gill, Wendy Lee, Sue Maggs, Lucy McKelvie,
Jenny Shapter, Janet Smith and Steven Wheeler
Recipes: Catherine Atkinson, Alex Barker, Carla Capalbo, Kit Chan, Maxine Clark,
Matthew Drennan, Christine France, Sarah Gates, Shirley Gill, Soheila Kimberley,
Lesley Mackley, Norma MacMillan, Jenny Stacey, Hilaire Walden, Steven Wheeler
and Jeni Wright

Printed and bound in Hong Kong/China

1 3 5 7 9 10 8 6 4 2

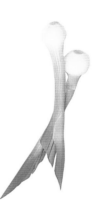

CONTENTS

INTRODUCTION

Packed with high-quality protein, meat is an excellent food. Careful rearing means leaner animals and hence healthier cuts, making it perfectly possible to follow current dietary advice while still enjoying meat and poultry.

A good butcher is the cook's best ally. Sensing this, most supermarkets have resident butchers to advise on cuts and cooking methods, and to prepare specialities such as rolled and stuffed loin of pork. Local butchers often prove even more helpful, getting to know their customers' likes and dislikes.

Lean fresh meat is easy to identify—unlike processed foods or pastries, which often have hidden fat, with meat the maxim is, what you see is what you get. If obvious fat has been removed and the meat looks lean, it *is* lean.

Poultry is available in a wide array of packaging, from parts such as breasts, thighs or drumsticks to whole birds. You can buy parts on or off the bone; with or without the skin; spiced, seasoned or marinated. Whole chickens are frequently flavored with lemon, herbs or garlic. Turkey is inexpensive and very versatile—cubes can often be substituted for red meat in casseroles, while breasts make excellent scallops. Duck breasts are delicious.

Making meat part of a healthy diet is largely a question of balance. It is not necessary to eat vast quantities—a simple salad, satay or stir-fry will deliver plenty of flavor with the minimum of meat. Family favorites like Chili con Carne, Irish Stew, fruity Lamb Tagine and Cassoulet may have originally evolved with economy in view, but the way they match small amounts of meat with generous quantities of vegetables, fruit, beans or pasta makes them perfect for today's healthier lifestyle.

Meat and Poultry Cuts

Shopping for meat can be bewildering. The range of cuts is wider than ever, with a proliferation of packaging offering portions of various sizes, many of them trimmed to meet the demand for leaner meat. Meat is marinated, spiced, supplied with sauces; available whole, sliced or diced. Recipes indicate which cut to choose, but if you are in any doubt, ask the butcher.

CHICKEN
Roast chicken makes a tasty and economical meal, especially if the carcass is used to make soup. Choose free-range birds for the best flavor. Cuts include breasts, legs, wings and thighs. Boneless thighs or breasts are a good buy.

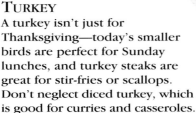

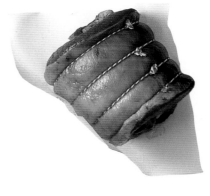

DUCK
There isn't a lot of meat on a duck, so buy large rather than small birds. Although leaner than it used to be, duck is still a fatty meat, so prick birds thoroughly all over before roasting. (You may have to drain off some of the fat from the roasting pan halfway through cooking.) Breasts are excellent for quick cooking methods, such as grilling and panfrying.

TURKEY
A turkey isn't just for Thanksgiving—today's smaller birds are perfect for Sunday lunches, and turkey steaks are great for stir-fries or scallops. Don't neglect diced turkey, which is good for curries and casseroles.

PHEASANT
Pheasant is seasonal. Find it at specialty butcher shops. Hens are generally held to be the most tender.

BEEF CUTS
Bone-in and boneless cuts are sold by weight, some with a thin layer of added fat to keep the meat moist during cooking. Short loin, rib, sirloin and fillet, or tenderloin, are best for roasting (fillet is particularly good in a pastry crust); chuck and rump are better pot-roasted.

BEEF STEAKS
Sirloin scores high in terms of flavor, while top loin is generally more tender and fillet almost melts in the mouth. The best steaks come from a butcher who really knows his trade. For Beef Olives, ask for thin slices of top round cut across the grain.

GROUND BEEF

Wonderfully versatile. Generally speaking, the paler the meat, the higher the fat content. Lean ground beef (such as ground sirloin or round) is widely available. Read the label and be sure to observe the "use by" date.

STEWING BEEF

The best cuts for stewing are neck, blade, chuck, flank, rump, shank and skirt.

CALF'S LIVER

Tender, economical and highly nutritious, calf's liver is also highly perishable, so use it as soon as possible after purchase.

STORING MEAT IN THE REFRIGERATOR OR FREEZER

Get meat home and into the refrigerator as soon as possible. Sealed packages should be left closed; wrapped meat should be put in a large container with a lid. Keep the meat on a low shelf and make sure it cannot drip onto any other food. Freeze only fresh meat, and do so as soon as possible after purchase. Always thaw frozen meat thoroughly before cooking.

LAMB ROASTS

Whole leg of lamb is the favorite roasting cut, although shoulder is more economical. Pot-roasting works well for leg of lamb.

GROUND LAMB

Ground lamb is the essential choice for classic Mediterranean dishes, such as Moussaka and Pastitsio, and for traditional dishes, such as Shepherd's Pie.

STEWING LAMB

The best cuts for stewing are neck, shoulder, breast, and sirloin chops. Trim off any excess fat before using in slow-cooked stews and casseroles.

PORK/HAM

For roasting, choose leg or loin. Pork cured in brine is called ham. Baked ham is delicious, especially with a classic Cumberland sauce.

SPARERIBS

Cut from the side or belly, these bones have small portions of very tasty meat. Usually baked, broiled or barbecued in a spicy sauce.

BACON

Used in meat cooking to add flavor or as a wrap to keep meat moist during cooking. Lean bacon is best for this. Bacon can be bought sliced thick or thin, or in a slab, which is ideal for making lardons (thin strips or dice).

SAUSAGES

The range is vast. Aside from regular pork or beef sausages, there are country-style variations that include herbs, leeks, cheese or other fillings. Pepperoni (above) is a small, firm, spicy sausage that is a favorite with pizza lovers.

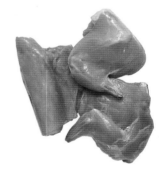

RABBIT

This often underrated meat is low in fat and has an excellent flavor. It makes a fine pie.

Flavorings and Oils

You don't need a vast pantry to be a successful cook, but a few carefully selected flavorings and the right oils can make all the difference to your favorite dishes.

Anchovies

These canned fish have been filleted and salted before being packed in oil. They are traditional partners for several meat dishes, either as a garnish or in sauces, in which they dissolve to enrich the flavor.

Passata

Smooth and full-flavored, this is sieved puréed tomatoes. Use it as the basis of soups, casseroles, pot roasts or pasta sauces. Sold in jars and cartons, it should be kept in the refrigerator after opening and used as soon as possible.

Soy Sauce

Made from fermented soybeans, soy sauce is available in dark and light varieties. Dark soy sauce has a richer flavor and is widely used in marinades, sauces and stir-fries. Use light soy sauce when only a hint of soy flavor is required. Soy sauce is salty, so check before adding extra salt.

Sun-dried Tomato Paste

Sun-dried tomato paste is richer and has a fuller flavor than regular tomato paste or purée.

Sun-dried Tomatoes

A popular ingredient, sun-dried tomatoes have a concentrated flavor that really peps up stews and ground meat mixtures. Sun-dried tomatoes preserved in oil are ready to use; dried tomatoes must be soaked in water first.

Extra Virgin Olive Oil

First-pressing olive oil is a lovely, rich, green color and has a wonderful taste. It is superb in salads and on pasta, but the flavor can be somewhat overwhelming; for frying, use a light olive oil or mix it with sunflower oil. Olive oils are like wines—they vary enormously from producer to producer and year to year. If you find one that really suits your palate, stick with it.

Above, from left: Dark sesame oil, sun-dried tomatoes in oil, canned anchovies in oil and light soy sauce.

Left, from left: Passata, extra virgin olive oil, sun-dried tomato paste and sunflower oil.

Dark Sesame Oil

A few drops of this flavorful oil, added to stir-fries, marinades, dressings, noodles or pasta just before serving, really boosts the taste. Don't use it for frying, as it burns at a low temperature.

Sunflower Oil

This light oil has no flavor of its own and is ideal for frying. It can be mixed with more highly flavored oils, such as extra virgin olive oil.

Herbs and Spices

The judicious use of herbs and spices makes all the difference to meat cookery.

Bouquet Garni

A popular flavoring for stews and casseroles, a bouquet garni classically consists of a bay leaf and a sprig each of parsley and thyme, tied in cheesecloth or bound with kitchen string. A length of leek or celery is sometimes added. Tie the end of the string to the pan handle for easy removal.

Caraway Seeds

Small brown seeds with a warm, pungent, anise flavor. They combine well with pork as well as potatoes, cabbage, onions and cheese. Used in both sweet and savory dishes.

Chiles, Chili Powder and Crushed Dried Chiles

There are scores of varieties of fresh chiles, ranging from mild to fiery, and shaped like miniature peppers or pods. To reduce the heat, remove the seeds before cooking. Chili powders come in various strengths, some with added herbs and spices. Crushed dried chiles are widely used in Indian dishes.

Dill Weed

Fresh dill is light and feathery. It looks pretty on the plate and imparts a delicate anise flavor. It is widely used in Scandinavian cooking.

Fresh Coriander (Cilantro), Coriander Seeds and Ground Coriander

Leaf coriander, known as cilantro, has a wonderful aroma. The taste is mild but distinctive—spicy and earthy. Sprinkle it over a dish at the end of cooking or use it as a garnish. Coriander seeds taste quite different. Dry-roasted and freshly ground, they have a heady aroma with a burnt-orange taste. Ground coriander is used in curries and tagines.

Ground Cumin and Cumin Seeds

Often used with ground coriander, cumin is another popular curry spice that also goes well with cheese, fish and vegetables. It has a strong, slightly bitter taste.

Ground Ginger/Fresh Ginger

Ground ginger is not widely used in meat cooking, but finds its way into some curry powders. Fresh ginger is a favorite Chinese ingredient, used as an aromatic in stir-fries and similar dishes. It is particularly good with chicken. Buy plump, smooth roots and store them, tightly wrapped, in the refrigerator for a few weeks, or in the freezer. Frozen ginger grates easily and thaws on contact with hot food.

Juniper Berries

The familiar flavoring in gin, juniper berries are used in meat cooking to add a rich, gamy taste. Crushing them releases their flavor fully.

Kaffir Lime Leaves

These aromatic leaves are dark green, shiny and joined in pairs. They are widely used in Indian, Indonesian and Thai dishes. Add them whole and remove them before serving, or chop them and incorporate them into the dish. Kaffir lime leaves can be difficult to track down; if you find a supply, buy plenty and store them in the freezer, wrapped in plastic.

Above, clockwise from top left: Bouquet garni, chiles (fresh, crushed, powder), juniper berries, kaffir lime leaves, turmeric, oregano (fresh, dried), fresh dill, cilantro, coriander (seeds, ground), caraway seeds. *Center*: Cumin (ground, seeds), ginger (ground, fresh).

Oregano

Synonymous with Italian and Greek cooking, this herb has a distinctive, pungent flavor.

Turmeric

An aromatic ground spice that imparts a brilliant yellow color to food. It is one of the ingredients in curry powder.

Equipment

Sharp knives and good pans are probably top of the list of desirable items when it comes to cooking meat, but there are several other pieces of equipment that will make your task easier.

Casseroles

Flameproof casseroles are the best choice for making stews and pot roasts, as they can be used on the stove for browning meat or vegetables before being transferred to the oven for slow cooking.

Colanders

Metal colanders are invaluable for draining large quantities of food, like potatoes, pasta or rice. Draining browned ground meat or meat cubes in a colander gets rid of excess fat and makes for healthier casseroles, stews and sauces.

Cutters

Metal cutters make short work of cutting out pastry or bread circles for pies or for croûtes.

Cutting Boards

Have at least two rigid nylon boards, reserving one for cutting raw meat and poultry. Wash them thoroughly after every use.

Grater

A good-quality, freestanding box grater with serrations of different sizes is essential, not only for cheese and vegetables, but also for grating ginger. You can even use a grater to make bread crumbs, if you don't have a food processor.

Grinder

If you grind your own meat, you control how lean it is. Nothing beats an old-fashioned kitchen grinder with a selection of blades for varying the texture. A food processor can be used in a pinch, but the meat will be finely chopped, not ground.

Knives

Good knives are a cook's best friend. It pays to buy the highest quality you can afford. For starters, invest in a cook's knife with a heavy, wide blade about seven inches long. This is ideal for cutting meat. Paring knives—small knives with short, sharp blades—are ideal for vegetables. Buy several. There's nothing worse than having to turn down offers of help in the kitchen because you only have one decent knife!

Loaf Pan

For making meat loaf and terrines, a good-quality loaf pan is needed. Line the bottom with baking parchment before adding the mixture.

Measuring Cups and Spoons

Use graduated measures for stocks and sauces, and proper measuring spoons rather than inaccurate kitchen cutlery.

Mixing Bowls

Buy several sizes, including a large bowl for making pastry.

Mixing Spoons

Rigid plastic spoons are preferred, as they do not absorb flavors from the food.

Muffin Pans

Useful for making muffins, Yorkshire puddings or popovers.

Pastry Brush

A small but useful utensil, this can be used to oil roasting pans and baking dishes or pans, glaze pastry with milk or beaten egg or brush the last traces of cheese or lemon rind from a grater.

Above, from top left: Colander, loaf pans, grater, sieves, mixing bowls, casserole, thermometer. *On the muffin pan*: Knives, pastry brush, mixing spoon. *On the cutting board*: Cutters, grinder, garlic press and salt and pepper mills.

Pots and Pans

It pays to buy good-quality pans, even if you start with a cheaper set and replace them one at a time. If you like slow-cooked stews, make sure you have a pan with a thick, solid bottom that will allow you to simmer the food without scorching it. Read the labels on any pans you buy—some new pans hold the heat so well that it is vital to turn the heat down once their contents

come to a boil. Other pans may need seasoning before use.

A wok is invaluable for stir-frying and steaming. Choose a flat-bottomed wok if you are cooking on an electric stove, or the pan will wobble dangerously on the burner and will not heat up correctly.

You will need at least two frying pans, including a small one and a larger, deep frying pan that comes with a lid.

Mortar and Pestle

This is the perfect tool for grinding spices. Dry-roast the spices first for optimum flavor. Choose a small mortar and pestle for grinding small amounts of dry spices, and a larger version for pounding such "wet" ingredients as fresh ginger.

Roasting Pans

Rather than buy two roasting pans of the same size, choose one that will amply accommodate the Sunday roast, and a smaller pan for items like roasted vegetables or for Yorkshire pudding. Check that the pans are absolutely level. If you are replacing an existing roasting pan, do not throw the old pan away. Save it for the grill.

Slotted Spoon

One of the most useful kitchen utensils, this enables you to fish whole spices out of stews, transfer browned meat cubes from frying pan to casserole and drain deep-fried items.

Left, hanging: Large saucepan, frying pans. *Bottom row from left*: Roasting pans, nylon cutting board and heavy flameproof casserole.

Below, from left: Slotted spoons, mortars and pestles and heat-proof glass measuring cups.

TECHNIQUES

Trimming and Chopping Meat

Use a sharp cook's knife for preparing meat, and use a board kept especially for the purpose.

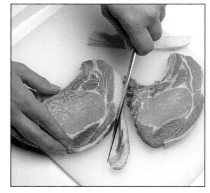

1 Preparing meat for stir-frying: Trim away any excess fat. Using a sharp knife, cut or chop the meat as required for the recipe. Keep the pieces fairly small and of uniform size, so they take the same time to cook.

2 Trimming pork chops: Use a sharp knife to cut away any rind and excess fat, leaving a little of the fat in place if the chops are to be broiled. Snip this fat several times with scissors to prevent it from curling during cooking.

3 Trimming lamb chops: Trim off excess fat with a sharp knife, then cut and scrape away all fat and gristle from the ends of the protruding bones. Cover the bone ends with foil to prevent charring.

Preparing Veal and Poultry Scallops

Scallops are beaten-out portions of veal or poultry that are crumbed and then shallow-fried.

1 Veal scallops: Trim any fat and gristle from around the edge of the veal scallops (½-inch slices from the fillet end of the leg). Place the slices in turn between sheets of plastic wrap. Using the smooth side of a meat mallet or the roller of a rolling pin, pound the meat gently but firmly all over to flatten it to a thickness of about ⅛ inch. It will very nearly double in size.

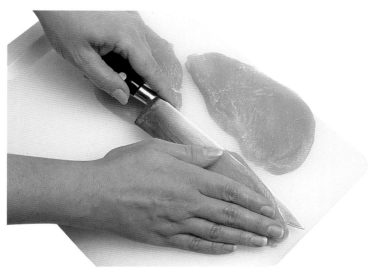

2 Poultry scallops: Chicken or turkey breast fillets can be treated in exactly the same way. If the breasts are very thick, slice them horizontally in half before pounding them.

Preparing Meat for Roasting

Roasts are sold ready for the oven, but you may want to give the meat a special treatment to boost the flavor.

Stuffing and Trussing a Chicken

Trussing a chicken, especially if it is stuffed, maintains its shape and ensures that the stuffing doesn't escape.

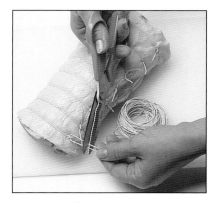

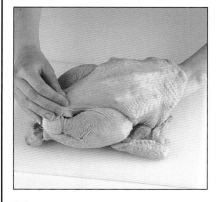

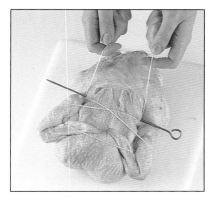

1 Tying a boned roast: If you stuff a boned roast yourself, it will need to be rolled and tied before cooking. Reshape the meat neatly, make sure any stuffing is evenly distributed, then bind with butcher's string at 1-inch intervals.

2 Preparing a leg of lamb for roasting: Rub the leg with oil or butter and season with pepper. For extra flavor, make tiny slits in the surface of the roast and insert a sliver of garlic and a fresh rosemary leaf in each. Alternatively, use slices of fresh ginger with lime rind.

1 Stuff the small neck end of the bird, not the large cavity, as the heat from the oven may not penetrate this area. Do not pack the stuffing too tightly. Fold the neck flap neatly under the chicken and tuck the wing tips under to hold the flap in place.

2 With the chicken on its back, press the legs down to improve the shape. Push a skewer through the bird, below the thigh bone, then turn it over. Loop string round the wings, crossing it over, then pass the string under the ends of the skewer.

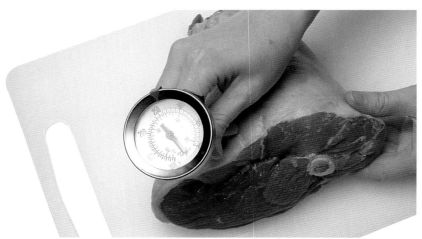

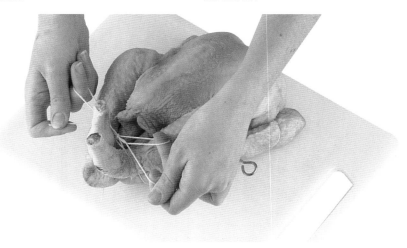

3 Insert a meat thermometer through the thickest part of the roast, without touching the bone. Roast for the recommended time; for pink lamb, the temperature should be 135°F; for well-done meat, it should reach 160°F.

3 Crisscross the string over the back of the chicken, then, still holding the ends of the string, carefully turn the bird over onto its back. Bring the string up to tie the drumsticks and the parson's nose together neatly.

Cutting Up a Chicken

For casseroles, it is often more economical to buy a whole chicken and cut it up yourself, rather than buy chicken parts.

Grinding Meat

A wide range of ground meat is available, but for special mixtures it is often desirable to grind your own.

1 Holding the chicken firmly, cut the skin between the leg and breast. Press the leg down to expose the ball-and-socket joint, cut or break the joint apart and cut down toward the parson's nose to release the leg joint. Repeat on the other side.

2 Feel for the end of the breastbone, and cut diagonally through to the rib cage. Use a pair of poultry shears or strong kitchen scissors to cut through the rib cage and wishbone, separating the two wing joints.

1 A grinder produces the most uniform ground meat, and you can vary the texture, depending on which blade is used. Trim the meat well, cut it into 1½-inch cubes or strips, then feed it through the machine.

2 A food processor will produce a somewhat different result, chopping rather than grinding the meat. Trim the meat and remove all gristle, then cut it into cubes. Fit a metal blade in the processor, add the meat and chop, using the pulsing action.

3 With clean hands, gently twist the wing tip (pinion) and tuck it under the breast meat on each wing joint in turn so that the joint is held flat. This gives it a good shape for cooking. Cut the leg joints in half if you like.

4 Use the shears to cut the breast meat from the carcass in one piece, so that all that remains is half the rib cage and the backbone, with the parson's nose attached. Cut the breast in two pieces, through the breastbone, if you like.

3 When the machine is switched off between pulses, stir the meat around so that it will be chopped evenly. Take care not to process the meat to a purée, particularly if making hamburgers, or they will be tough.

4 If you have neither grinder nor food processor, cubed meat can be minced by hand. Use a large chef's knife. Holding the tip of the blade down, raise and lower the knife by the handle, changing the position often, until the meat is fairly finely chopped.

Marinating Meat

Marinating is the soaking of food such as poultry or meat in a moist mixture prior to cooking, and is usually done to ensure that the food does not dry out when broiled or grilled. As a bonus, marinades tenderize and add flavor.

1 Place the food for marinating in a shallow bowl or dish, large enough to hold all the pieces in a single layer. If marinating a large piece, use a dish that will hold it fairly snugly.

2 Mix the marinade. An oil-based marinade is used for dry meats such as poultry; a wine or vinegar-based marinade is used for rich meats with a higher fat content.

3 Pour the marinade over the food, then turn the portions with tongs to coat them evenly. If there are herbs in the marinade, make sure they are evenly distributed.

4 Cover the dish and set it aside. If marinating for more than 30 minutes, put the dish in the refrigerator. Turn the portions occasionally, spooning the marinade over them.

5 Lift out the marinated food, drain it and reserve or discard the marinade, according to the recipe. If necessary, let the food come to room temperature before cooking.

6 The marinade can be used for basting or brushing food during cooking, but take care if using an oil-based marinade on grilled food, as it could cause flare-ups.

QUICK MARINADES

For meat, mix 3 tablespoons each of sunflower oil and dry sherry with 1 tablespoon each of Worcestershire sauce and dark soy sauce. Add crushed garlic and pepper.

For poultry, mix ½ cup dry white wine with 4 tablespoons olive oil, 1 tablespoon lemon juice and 2 tablespoons chopped fresh herbs. Add pepper to taste.

Browning Meat Cubes for Stewing

Starting a stew by searing the meat ensures that the flavor is sealed in; long, slow cooking produces a tender result.

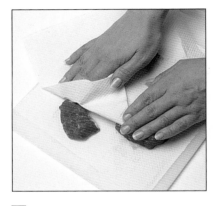

1 Trim the meat and cut it into cubes or strips, as required for the recipe. Pat dry with paper towels. If the meat needs to be coated in seasoned flour, do this in a strong plastic bag.

2 Heat a little oil in a frying pan or flameproof casserole until very hot. Fry a few cubes at a time until browned on all sides. As each cube browns, lift it out of the pan.

3 Cook any vegetables required in the fat remaining in the pan, then drain off the excess oil. Return the browned meat cubes to the pan and mix well.

4 Pour in liquid to cover and stir to mix. Add any herbs or flavorings and bring the liquid to a boil. Lower the heat, cover and simmer the stew for the time suggested in the recipe.

Dry-frying Ground Meat

Dry-frying is an excellent way of sealing ground meat at the start of cooking, since it uses the meat's own fat and does not require any oil.

1 Heat a nonstick frying pan gently over a low flame.

2 Add the ground meat, spreading it out with a plastic spoon to cover the bottom of the pan.

3 Sauté the meat for about 5 minutes, or until it is evenly browned all over. If there is any excess fat, pour it off.

Pan-frying Steaks

Tender cuts of meat, such as sirloin or fillet steak, are ideal for pan-frying. Use the meat juices as the basis for a sauce.

1 Trim the steaks, leaving a little fat around the edge, if you like, and pat them dry with paper towels. If using a coating, such as crushed peppercorns, press this evenly on both sides of the meat.

2 Heat the fat (a mixture of butter and oil works well) in a frying pan. When it is hot, add the steaks in a single layer, taking care not to crowd the pan.

3 Sear the steaks quickly on both sides, then lower the heat fractionally and cook the steaks on both sides until done to your taste. For a rare steak, allow 2–3 minutes a side.

Stir-frying

Meat for stir-frying should be cut into small cubes or strips of uniform size. In view of the short cooking time, a tender cut must be used.

1 Heat a wok or large, deep frying pan over moderately high heat. When the wok or pan is hot, dribble a ring of oil around the inner rim, so that it coats the sides.

2 Flavor the oil with aromatics, such as garlic, ginger or sesame seeds, if you like. Add the beef pieces, in batches if necessary. Cook them quickly, using a spatula to turn them over.

3 Add ingredients like snow peas, which need less cooking time, toward the end. Toss them with the meat until they are crisp-tender. Add any sauce as specified in individual recipes.

Braising Chicken

One-pot meals are easy and convenient, and the long, slow cooking means that the flavors blend beautifully as the meat cooks to perfection.

1 Heat olive oil in a flameproof casserole. When it is hot, add the chicken pieces, in batches if necessary. Fry, turning several times, until browned all over. Add stock, wine or a mixture of both to a depth of about 1 inch.

2 Tuck in a bouquet garni or add chopped herbs, season and bring to a boil. Lower the heat, cover and cook on the stove or in a preheated 350°F oven for 1½ hours, until tender.

3 Add a selection of lightly sautéed vegetables about halfway through cooking. Glazed button onions, mushrooms, carrots and small new potatoes would make a good mixture.

Pot-roasting

Prime cuts can be pot-roasted, but this method really comes into its own for those flavorful, less tender cuts that benefit from being seared, then cooked slowly in stock.

1 If necessary, tie the meat into a good shape. Pat it dry with paper towels. Heat a little oil in a flameproof casserole. When it is very hot, add the meat (or poultry) and fry until well browned all over, turning it with two spatulas.

2 Add a small amount of stock or a mixture of stock and wine. Heat, stirring in any browned bits that have accumulated on the bottom of the pot.

3 Arrange the vegetables around the meat. Add the remaining liquid, with seasonings or herbs. Bring to a boil, cover and simmer for 2½ – 3 hours, until the meat is tender. Lift out the meat and vegetables, skim the cooking juices and boil them rapidly to make gravy.

Roasting a Chicken

Chickens have very little fat. The breast can dry out if not protected during roasting. A little butter not only keeps the bird moist, but also helps to crisp the skin.

Carving Chicken and Lamb

Roast poultry and meat should be left to stand under tented foil for 10–15 minutes after roasting before being carved to allow the juices to "settle" and make carving easier.

1 Preheat the oven to 375°F. Rinse the chicken inside and out, then pat it dry. Season the cavity, then stuff the neck end, if you like. Spread the breast lightly with butter; place the bird on a rack over a roasting pan.

2 Roast the chicken for 20 minutes per pound, plus another 20 minutes. After the first 30 minutes, baste the bird every 10–15 minutes with the juices in the pan. If the breast starts to brown too quickly, cover it with foil.

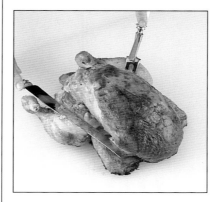 

1 Carving chicken: Holding the bird firmly with a carving fork, use a carving knife to cut between the leg and breast. Press the leg down to expose the joint, then cut through. Slip the knife under the back to remove the "oyster" with the leg.

2 With the knife at the top end of the breastbone, cut down parallel on one side of the wishbone to take a good slice of breast meat with the wing. As you remove the pieces, arrange them neatly on a heated serving platter.

3 To test that the chicken is cooked, pierce the thickest part of the thigh with the point of a sharp knife. The juices that run out should be clear. If there is any trace of pink, roast the chicken for 10 minutes more and test again. Transfer the cooked chicken to a carving board and let it rest under tented foil for 10–15 minutes before carving.

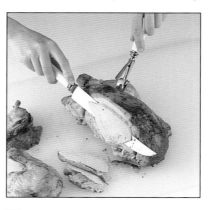 

3 Place the knife at the end of the breastbone and carefully cut down the front of the carcass to remove the wishbone. Hold the knife at a slight angle and cut the remaining breast meat into neat slices.

4 Carving a leg of lamb: With the thicker area uppermost, cut a wedge-shaped slice from the wider edge. This makes subsequent slicing easier. Continue to slice the meat at a slight angle down toward the bone, against the grain, then carve the other side.

Chicken and Leek Soup

A chunky chicken and vegetable soup served with garlic-flavored fried croutons—a meal in itself.

Serves 4

INGREDIENTS
4 boned and skinned chicken thighs
1 tablespoon butter
2 small leeks, thinly sliced
2 tablespoons long-grain rice
3¾ cups chicken stock
1 tablespoon chopped mixed fresh
    parsley and mint
salt and freshly ground black pepper
crusty bread, to serve

FOR THE GARLIC CROUTONS
2 tablespoons olive oil
1 garlic clove, crushed
4 slices of bread, cut into cubes

parsley *mint*

long-grain rice

garlic

olive oil

bread

chicken thighs

butter

leeks

1 Cut the chicken into ½-inch cubes. Melt the butter in a saucepan, add the leeks and cook until tender. Add the long-grain rice and chicken and cook for another 2 minutes.

2 Add the stock, then cover and simmer for 15–20 minutes, until tender.

COOK'S TIP
To make this soup more economical, buy chicken thighs or parts with the bones and skin still intact and prepare them yourself.

3 To make the garlic croutons, heat the oil in a large frying pan. Add the crushed garlic clove and bread cubes and cook until golden brown, stirring all the time to prevent them from burning. Drain the croutons on paper towels and sprinkle with a little salt.

4 Add the parsley and mint to the soup and adjust the seasoning. Garnish with some garlic croutons, then serve with the remaining croutons passed separately and some crusty bread.

Mulligatawny Soup

The English army brought back the recipe for this curried chicken and rice soup from India in the eighteenth century.

Serves 4

INGREDIENTS
4 tablespoons butter or
    4 tablespoons oil
2 large chicken pieces, about
    12 ounces each
1 onion, chopped
1 carrot, chopped
1 small rutabaga, chopped
about 1 tablespoon curry powder,
    to taste
4 cloves
6 black peppercorns, lightly crushed
¼ cup lentils
3¾ cups chicken stock
¼ cup golden raisins
salt and freshly ground black pepper

butter
cloves
carrot
chicken
curry powder
onion
rutabaga
chicken stock
black peppercorns
lentils

1 Melt the butter or heat the oil in a large saucepan, then cook the chicken over brisk heat until browned. Transfer the chicken to a plate.

2 Add the onion, carrot and rutabaga to the saucepan and cook, stirring occasionally, until the vegetables are lightly colored. Stir in the curry powder, cloves and black peppercorns and cook for 1–2 minutes, then add the lentils. Pour the chicken stock into the saucepan, bring to a boil, then add the golden raisins and chicken and any juices from the plate. Cover and simmer gently for about 1¼ hours.

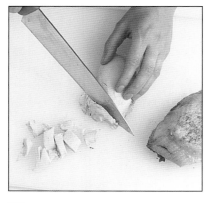

3 Remove the chicken from the pan and discard the skin and bones. Chop the flesh, return to the soup and reheat. Check the seasoning before serving the soup piping hot.

COOK'S TIP
Choose red split lentils for the best color, although either green or brown lentils could also be used.

VARIATION
If rutabaga is out of season or unavailable, substitute about 3 small white turnips, or use 2–3 extra carrots instead.

Blue Cheese Burger Salad with Sesame Croutons

The beefy hamburgers contain a surprise layer of Roquefort cheese at the center.

Serves 4

INGREDIENTS
2 pounds lean ground beef
1 egg
1 onion, finely chopped
2 teaspoons Dijon mustard
½ teaspoons celery salt
4 ounces Roquefort or other blue cheese
1 large sesame seed loaf
3 tablespoons olive oil
1 small head of iceberg lettuce
2 ounces (about ½ bunch) arugula or watercress
½ cup French dressing
4 ripe tomatoes, quartered
4 large scallions, sliced
freshly ground black pepper

arugula rocket

olive oil

ground beef

onion

tomatoes

egg

sesame seed loaf

Dijon mustard

iceberg lettuce

scallions

Roquefort cheese

1 Place the ground beef, egg, onion, mustard, celery salt and pepper in a mixing bowl. Combine thoroughly. Divide the mixture into 16 portions.

2 Flatten the pieces between two sheets of plastic wrap or waxed paper to form 5-inch rounds.

3 Place ½ ounce of the cheese on eight of the thin burgers. Sandwich with the remainder and press the edges firmly. Store the burgers between pieces of plastic wrap or waxed paper and chill until ready to cook.

4 To make the sesame croutons, preheat the broiler. Remove the sesame crust from the bread, then cut the crust into short fingers. Moisten with olive oil and toast evenly for 10–15 minutes.

5 Season the burgers and broil for about 10 minutes, turning once.

6 Wash the salad greens and spin or pat dry on paper towels. Toss with the dressing, then distribute among four large plates. Place two burgers in the center of each plate and arrange the tomatoes, scallions and sesame croutons around the edge.

Warm Duck Salad with Orange and Coriander

The rich, gamy flavor of duck provides the foundation for this delicious late-summer salad.

Serves 4

INGREDIENTS
1 small orange
2 boneless duck breasts
²⁄₃ cup dry white wine
1 teaspoon ground coriander seeds
½ teaspoon ground cumin or
    fennel seeds
2 tablespoons sugar
juice of ½ small lime or lemon
3 ounces day-old bread,
    thickly sliced
3 tablespoons olive oil
½ head of escarole
½ head of frisée
2 tablespoons sunflower or peanut oil
salt and cayenne pepper
4 sprigs cilantro, to garnish

orange
lime
cilantro
bread
escarole
duck breasts
frisée
olive oil
sunflower oil
dry white wine
sugar

1 Halve the orange and slice thickly. Discard any stray seeds and place the slices in a small saucepan. Cover with water, bring to a boil and simmer for 5 minutes to remove the bitterness. Drain and set aside.

2 Pierce the skin of the duck breasts diagonally with a small knife (this will help release the fat as they cook). Rub the skin with salt. Place a steel or cast-iron frying pan over steady heat and cook the breasts for 20 minutes, turning once, until they are medium rare. Transfer to a warm plate, cover and keep warm. Pour the duck fat into a small bowl and set aside for use on another occasion.

3 Heat the sediment in the pan until it begins to caramelize. Add the wine and stir to loosen the sediment. Add the coriander, cumin, sugar and orange slices. Boil quickly and reduce to a coating consistency. Sharpen with lime juice and season to taste.

4 To make the garlic croutons, remove the crusts from the bread and discard them. Cut the bread into short fingers. Heat the olive oil in a heavy frying pan, add the bread fingers and sauté, until evenly brown and crisp. Season with salt, then turn out onto paper towels to drain.

5 Wash the salad greens and spin or pat dry using paper towels. Moisten with sunflower oil and distribute among four large serving plates.

COOK'S TIP
Duck breast has the quality of red meat and is cooked either rare, medium or well done, according to taste.

6 Slice the duck breasts diagonally with a carving knife. Divide the breast meat into four portions and lift onto each salad plate. Spoon the dressing over the top, sprinkle with croutons, garnish with a sprig of cilantro and serve.

Melon and Prosciutto Salad with Strawberry Salsa

Sections of cool, fragrant melon wrapped with slices of air-dried ham make this a delicious appetizer.

Serves 4

INGREDIENTS
1 large melon (see Cook's Tip)
6 ounces prosciutto or Serrano ham, thinly sliced

FOR THE SALSA
2 cups strawberries
1 teaspoon sugar
2 tablespoons sunflower oil
1 tablespoon orange juice
½ teaspoon finely grated orange rind
½ teaspoon finely grated fresh ginger
salt and freshly ground black pepper

melon *strawberries*

orange

sugar

sunflower oil *ginger*

prosciutto

1 Halve the melon and remove the seeds with a spoon. Cut the rind away with a paring knife, then slice the melon thickly. Chill until ready to serve.

2 To make the salsa, hull the strawberries and cut them into large pieces. Place the strawberries in a small mixing bowl with the sugar and crush them lightly to release the juices. Add the oil, orange juice, rind and ginger. Season with salt and a generous grinding of black pepper.

3 Arrange the melon on a serving plate, lay the ham over the top and serve with a bowl of salsa.

COOK'S TIP
Choose a ripe, flavorful melon, such as cantaloupe, charentais or galia. To check that the melon is ripe, press the end opposite the stalk—if ripe, it will give to gentle pressure. Or simply smell it—a ripe melon will have a strongly perfumed aroma.

Chicken Saté

Marinate the chicken in the sauce overnight to allow the flavors to penetrate.

Serves 4

INGREDIENTS
4 chicken breasts
lemon slices, to garnish
lettuce leaves and scallions,
    to serve

FOR THE SATÉ SAUCE
½ cup crunchy peanut butter
1 small onion, chopped
1 garlic clove, crushed
2 tablespoons chutney
4 tablespoons olive oil
1 teaspoon light soy sauce
2 tablespoons lemon juice
¼ teaspoon chili powder or
    cayenne pepper

chicken breasts   *onion*

garlic

peanut butter   *chutney*   *lemon*

olive oil

soy sauce

chili powder

COOK'S TIP
If you are using wooden skewers, soak them in warm water for at least 30 minutes before skewering the meat to prevent them from burning.

1 Put all the saté sauce ingredients into a food processor or blender and process until smooth. Spoon into a dish.

2 Remove all bone and skin from the chicken and cut into 1-inch cubes. Add to the saté sauce mixture and stir to coat the chicken pieces. Cover with plastic wrap and chill for at least 4 hours or, better still, overnight.

3 Preheat the broiler or grill. Thread the chicken pieces onto short skewers.

4 Cook for 10 minutes, turning the skewers several times and brushing occasionally with the saté sauce. Garnish with lemon slices and serve on a bed of lettuce with scallions.

Chicken Liver Pâté with Marsala

Although this pâté is quick and simple to make, it has a delicious—and quite sophisticated—flavor.

Serves 4

INGREDIENTS
12 ounces chicken livers, defrosted
    if frozen
½ pound (2 sticks) butter, softened
2 garlic cloves, crushed
1 tablespoon Marsala, brandy or
    medium-dry sherry
1 teaspoon chopped fresh sage
salt and freshly ground black pepper
8 sage leaves, to garnish
Melba toast, to serve

butter

garlic cloves

sage

Marsala

chicken livers

COOK'S TIP
To make Melba toast, cook medium-sliced bread until golden brown, then cut off the crusts and carefully cut each slice horizontally in two by slipping a large sharp knife between the toasted sides. Toast, cut side up, under low heat until the toast curls slightly and crisps.

1 Pick over the chicken livers, then rinse and dry with paper towels. Melt 2 tablespoons of the butter in a frying pan and fry the chicken livers with the crushed garlic over medium heat for about 5 minutes, or until they are firm but still pink in the middle.

2 Transfer the livers to a blender or food processor and add the Marsala and chopped sage.

3 Melt 10 tablespoons of the remaining butter in the frying pan, stirring to loosen any sediment, then pour into the blender or processor and process until smooth. Season well.

4 Spoon the pâté into four individual pots and smooth the surface. Melt the remaining butter in a separate pan and pour over the pâtés. Chill until set. Garnish with sage leaves and serve with triangles of Melba toast.

Chicken, Pork and Walnut Terrine

The pungent spices and wine complement the meaty flavors of this rich terrine.

Serves 8 – 10

INGREDIENTS
2 boneless chicken breasts
1 large garlic clove, crushed
½ slice of bread
1 egg
12 ounces bacon chops (the fattier the better), ground or finely chopped (available from specialty butchers; smoked pork chops can be substituted)
8 ounces chicken or turkey livers, finely chopped
¼ cup chopped walnuts, toasted
2 tablespoons sweet sherry or Madeira
½ teaspoon ground allspice
½ teaspoon cayenne pepper
pinch each of ground nutmeg and cloves
8 long, lean bacon strips
salt and freshly ground black pepper
endive leaves and chives, to garnish

garlic
chicken breasts
chicken livers
bread
sherry
walnuts
egg
bacon chops
lean bacon

1 Cut the chicken into thin strips and season lightly. Mash the garlic, bread and egg together. Work in the chopped pork (using your hands is the best way) and then the finely chopped livers. Stir in the walnuts, sherry or Madeira, spices and seasoning to taste.

2 Preheat the oven to 400°F. Line an 8½ x 4½ x 2½-inch loaf pan with bacon strips and pack in half the meat mixture.

3 Lay the chicken strips on top and spread the rest of the mixture over them. Cover the pan with lightly greased foil, seal and press down firmly. Place the terrine in a roasting pan half full of hot water. Bake for 1 – 1½ hours, or until firm to the touch.

4 Remove the terrine from the oven, place weights on the top and let cool completely. Drain off any excess fat or liquid while the terrine is still warm.

5 When the terrine is completely cool, turn it out onto a board and cut into thick slices. Serve, garnished with a few endive leaves and chives.

COOK'S TIP
If you wish to seal the terrine for longer storage, pour melted lard over the top while the terrine is still in its pan. Leave the lard to set and form a complete seal. Store the terrine in the refrigerator for up to five days.

Meatballs with Porcini and Parmesan

These meatballs may be eaten hot or cold, as a main course or with pasta or rice.

Serves 3–4 as a main course

INGREDIENTS

¼ ounce (2 tablespoons) dried
    porcini mushrooms
1 pound lean ground beef
2 garlic cloves, finely chopped
4 tablespoons chopped fresh parsley
3 tablespoons chopped fresh basil
1 egg
6 tablespoons fresh bread crumbs
2 tablespoons freshly grated
    Parmesan cheese
4 tablespoons olive oil
1 onion, very finely chopped
¼ cup dry white wine
salt and freshly ground black pepper
chopped fresh parsley and a sprig,
    to garnish

porcini mushrooms

egg

ground beef

garlic

basil

parsley

bread crumbs

Parmesan cheese

olive oil

dry white wine

onion

1 Soak the dried porcini mushrooms in ⅔ cup warm water for 15 minutes. Lift out of the water and chop finely. Strain the soaking water through paper towels and reserve.

2 In a mixing bowl, combine the beef with the mushrooms, garlic and herbs. Stir in the egg. Add the bread crumbs and Parmesan, and season with salt and pepper. Form the mixture into small balls 1½ inches in diameter.

3 Heat the oil in a large, heavy frying pan. Add the onion and cook over low heat until soft. Raise the heat and add the meatballs, rolling them often to brown them evenly on all sides. After about 5 minutes, add the reserved mushroom soaking liquid. Cook the meatballs for another 5–8 minutes, or until they are cooked through.

4 Remove the meatballs to a warmed serving plate with a slotted spoon or spatula. Add the wine to the pan and cook for 1–2 minutes, stirring to scrape up any residue on the bottom of the pan. Pour the sauce over the meatballs. Sprinkle with fresh parsley, and serve the dish immediately with a sprig of parsley on the side.

Beef Olives

With beef slices rolled around a mushroom and bacon filling, beef olives really do resemble their namesake.

Serves 4

INGREDIENTS

2 tablespoons butter
2 bacon strips, finely chopped
4 ounces mushrooms, chopped
1 tablespoon chopped fresh parsley
grated rind and juice of 1 lemon
2 cups fresh bread crumbs
1½ pounds beef top round, cut into
    8 thin slices
3 tablespoons all-purpose flour
3 tablespoons sunflower oil
2 onions, sliced
scant 2 cups beef stock
salt and freshly ground black pepper
chopped fresh parsley, to garnish
mashed potatoes and peas, to serve

bacon

 mushrooms

lemon

parsley bread crumbs

all-purpose flour butter

sunflower oil onion

beef stock

1 Preheat the oven to 325°F. Heat the butter in a small pan, add the bacon and mushrooms and sauté, stirring frequently, for about 3 minutes, until cooked and golden brown. Let cool, then mix with the parsley, lemon rind and juice and bread crumbs. Season with salt and plenty of pepper.

2 Spread an equal amount of the bread crumb mixture evenly over each of the beef slices, leaving a narrow border clear around the edge.

COOK'S TIP
At the end of cooking, the onions can be puréed in a food processor or blender with a little of the stock, then stirred back into the casserole to make a smooth sauce, if desired.

3 Roll up the slices neatly, tucking in the ends. Tie the rolls securely with fine string, then dip them in flour to coat lightly. Heat the oil in a heavy, shallow pan and cook the beef rolls until lightly browned. Remove the beef rolls from the pan and keep warm.

4 Add the onions to the pan and sauté until browned. Stir in the remaining flour and cook until lightly browned. Pour in the stock, then bring to a boil, stirring, and simmer for 2–3 minutes. Transfer the beef rolls to a casserole, pour the sauce over them, then cover and bake for 2 hours. Lift out the "olives" and remove the string. Return to the sauce and serve hot, garnished with parsley. Serve with mashed potatoes and peas.

Osso Buco

This famous Milanese dish is rich and hearty.
Serve with risotto or plain boiled rice.

Serves 4

INGREDIENTS
2 tablespoons all-purpose flour
4 pieces of osso buco (veal shanks)
2 small onions
2 tablespoons olive oil
1 large celery stalk, finely chopped
1 carrot, finely chopped
2 garlic cloves, finely chopped
1 can (14 ounces) chopped tomatoes
1¼ cups dry white wine
1¼ cups chicken or veal stock
1 strip of thinly pared lemon rind
2 bay leaves, plus extra to garnish
salt and freshly ground black pepper

FOR THE GREMOLATA
2 tablespoons finely chopped fresh
    flat-leaf parsley
finely grated rind of 1 lemon
1 garlic clove, finely chopped

all-purpose
flour

onions   olive oil

celery

chopped
tomatoes

lemon   dry white
              wine

parsley   carrot

chicken stock   garlic

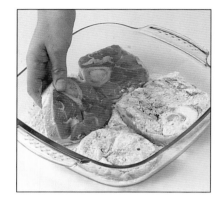

1 Preheat the oven to 325°F. Season the flour with salt and pepper and spread it out in a shallow dish. Add the pieces of osso buco and turn them in the flour until evenly coated. Shake off any excess flour.

2 Slice one of the onions and separate it into rings. Heat the oil in a large flameproof casserole, then add the veal, with the onion rings, and brown the veal on both sides over medium heat. Remove the veal shanks with tongs and set aside on paper towels to drain.

3 Chop the remaining onion and add it to the pan with the celery, carrot and garlic. Stir the bottom of the pan to incorporate the pan juices and sediment. Cook gently, stirring frequently, for about 5 minutes, until the vegetables begin to soften slightly.

4 Add the chopped tomatoes, wine, stock, lemon rind and bay leaves, then season to taste with salt and pepper. Bring to a boil, stirring. Return the veal to the pan and coat with the sauce. Cover and cook in the oven for 2 hours, or until the veal feels tender when pierced with a fork.

5 To make the gremolata, mix together the chopped parsley, lemon rind and garlic. Remove the casserole from the oven and lift out and discard the strip of lemon rind and the bay leaves. Taste the sauce for seasoning. Serve the osso buco hot, sprinkled with the gremolata and garnished with extra bay leaves.

Hungarian Beef Goulash

Beef goulash is a rich, warming stew that is flavored with the distinctive, pungent Hungarian spice paprika.

Serves 4

INGREDIENTS
2 tablespoons sunflower oil
2¼ pounds stewing beef, cubed
2 onions, chopped
1 garlic clove, crushed
1 tablespoon all-purpose flour
2 teaspoons paprika
1 teaspoon caraway seeds
1 can (14 ounces) chopped tomatoes
1¼ cups beef stock
1 large carrot, chopped
1 red bell pepper, seeded and chopped
sour cream and paprika, to garnish

FOR THE DUMPLINGS
1 cup self-rising flour
½ cup shredded suet or grated
    chilled shortening
1 tablespoon chopped fresh parsley
½ teaspoon caraway seeds
salt and freshly ground black pepper

sunflower oil
onions
beef stock
stewing beef
flour
paprika
garlic   carrot
chopped tomatoes
red bell pepper
self-rising flour
sour cream

1 Heat the oil in a large flameproof casserole, add the meat and sauté over high heat for 5 minutes, stirring, until browned. Remove with a slotted spoon.

2 Add the onions and garlic and sauté gently for 5 minutes, until softened. Add the flour, paprika and caraway seeds, stir and cook for 2 minutes. Return the browned meat to the casserole and stir in the chopped tomatoes and stock. Bring to a boil, cover and simmer gently for about 2 hours.

3 Meanwhile, make the dumplings. Sift the flour and seasoning into a bowl, add the suet, parsley, caraway seeds and 3–4 tablespoons water and mix to a soft dough. Divide into eight pieces and roll into balls. Cover and reserve.

4 After 2 hours, stir the carrot and pepper into the goulash and season well. Drop the dumplings into the goulash, cover and simmer for about 25 minutes. Serve in individual bowls topped with a spoonful of sour cream and sprinkled with a pinch of paprika.

Irish Stew

Tender, slow-cooked lamb and vegetables make this a welcome dish on a cold winter's night.

Serves 4

INGREDIENTS

4 lean bacon strips, chopped
2 celery stalks, chopped
2 large onions, sliced
8 shoulder lamb chops, about
    2¼ pounds total weight
2¼ pounds potatoes, sliced
1¼ cups beef stock or water
1½ tablespoons Worcestershire
    sauce
1 teaspoon anchovy sauce
salt and freshly ground black pepper
chopped fresh parsley, to garnish

bacon

celery

onions

beef stock

lamb chops

Worcestershire sauce

potatoes

1 Preheat the oven to 325°F. Fry the bacon for 3–5 minutes, until the fat runs, then add the celery and a third of the onions and cook, stirring occasionally, until browned.

2 Layer the lamb chops, potatoes, vegetables and bacon and remaining onions in a heavy flameproof casserole, seasoning each layer and finishing with a layer of potatoes.

3 Gently stir the stock or water, Worcestershire sauce and anchovy sauce into the bacon and vegetable cooking juices in the pan and bring to a boil. Pour into the casserole, adding water if necessary so the liquid comes halfway up the casserole.

4 Cover the casserole tightly, then transfer it to the oven and cook for 3 hours, or until the meat and vegetables are tender. Serve hot, sprinkled with chopped parsley.

COOK'S TIP

Mutton, which originally gave the flavor to Irish stew, is often difficult to obtain nowadays, so lamb is used instead and other flavorings are added to compensate for it.

Moussaka

A popular classic, this moussaka is mildly spiced and encased in a golden baked crust.

Serves 6

INGREDIENTS

2¼ pounds eggplant
½ cup olive oil
2 large tomatoes
2 large onions, sliced
1 pound ground lamb
¼ teaspoon ground cinnamon
¼ teaspoon ground allspice
2 tablespoons tomato paste
3 tablespoons chopped fresh parsley
½ cup dry white wine
salt and freshly ground black pepper

FOR THE SAUCE

4 tablespoons butter
½ cup all-purpose flour
2½ cups milk
¼ teaspoon grated nutmeg
⅓ cup grated Parmesan cheese
3 tablespoons toasted bread crumbs

eggplant

olive oil   *parsley*

tomato paste   *ground lamb*

milk

butter   *flour*

Parmesan cheese

onions

dry white wine

tomatoes

1 Cut the eggplant into ¼-inch-thick slices. Layer the slices in a colander, sprinkling each layer with plenty of salt. Let stand for 30 minutes.

2 Rinse the eggplant in several changes of cold water. Squeeze slices gently with your fingers to remove any excess water, then pat them dry on paper towels. Heat some of the oil in a large frying pan. Fry the eggplant slices in batches until golden on both sides, adding more oil when necessary. Let the fried eggplant slices drain on paper towels while you cook the rest.

3 Plunge the tomatoes into boiling water for about 30 seconds, then refresh in cold water. Peel away the skins and chop the tomatoes roughly.

4 Preheat the oven to 350°F. Heat 2 tablespoons oil in a large saucepan. Add the onions and ground lamb and sauté gently for 5 minutes, stirring and breaking up the lamb with a wooden spoon as it cooks.

5 Add the tomatoes, cinnamon, allspice, tomato paste, parsley, wine and pepper and bring to a boil. Reduce the heat, cover with a lid and simmer gently for 15 minutes.

6 Put alternate layers of the eggplant and meat mixture in a shallow ovenproof dish, finishing with a layer of eggplant.

7 To make the sauce, melt the butter in a small pan and stir in the flour. Cook, stirring, for 1 minute. Remove from the heat and gradually blend in the milk. Return to the heat and cook, stirring, for 2 minutes, until thickened. Add the nutmeg, cheese and salt and pepper. Pour the sauce over the eggplant and sprinkle with the bread crumbs. Bake for 45 minutes, until golden. Serve hot, sprinkled with extra black pepper.

Lamb Tagine

Combining meat, dried fruit and spices is typical of Moroccan cooking. "Tagine" is the name of both the stew and the traditional pot it is cooked in.

Serves 4–6

INGREDIENTS

½ cup dried apricots
2 tablespoons olive oil
1 large onion, chopped
2¼ pounds boneless shoulder of
    lamb, cubed
1 teaspoon ground cumin
1 teaspoon ground coriander
1 teaspoon ground cinnamon
grated rind and juice of ½ orange
1 teaspoon saffron strands
1 tablespoon ground almonds
about 1¼ cups lamb or chicken
    stock
1 tablespoon sesame seeds
salt and freshly ground black pepper
fresh parsley, to garnish
couscous, to serve

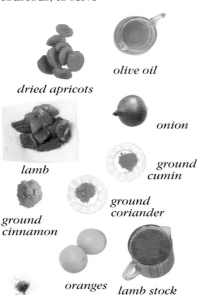

dried apricots

olive oil

lamb

onion

ground cinnamon

ground cumin

ground coriander

saffron

oranges

lamb stock

almonds

1 Cut the apricots in half and put in a bowl with ⅔ cup water. Let soak overnight.

2 Preheat the oven to 350°F. Heat the olive oil in a flameproof casserole. Add the onion and cook gently for 10 minutes, until soft and golden.

3 Stir in the lamb. Add the ground cumin, coriander and cinnamon, with salt and pepper to taste. Stir to coat the lamb cubes in the spices. Cook, stirring, for 5 minutes.

COOK'S TIP
If you do not have time to soak the apricots, use the ready-to-eat variety and add extra stock to replace the soaking liquid.

4 Add the apricots and their soaking liquid. Stir in the orange rind and juice, saffron, ground almonds and enough stock to cover. Cover the casserole and cook in the oven for 1 – 1½ hours, until the meat is tender, stirring occasionally and adding more stock if necessary.

5 Heat a heavy frying pan. Add the sesame seeds and dry-fry in the pan until golden. Sprinkle the sesame seeds over the meat, garnish with parsley and serve with couscous.

Chili Con Carne

Simple and economical, this spicy dish is one of the most popular ground beef recipes.

Serves 4

INGREDIENTS

1 tablespoon sunflower oil
8 ounces ground beef
1 onion, quartered
1 teaspoon chili powder
2 tablespoons all-purpose flour
2 tablespoons tomato paste
²⁄₃ cup beef stock
7-ounce can chopped tomatoes
7-ounce can kidney beans, drained
1 green bell pepper, seeded
    and chopped
1 tablespoon Worcestershire sauce
½ cup long-grain rice
salt and freshly ground black pepper
sour cream and chopped fresh
    parsley, to garnish

sunflower oil

ground beef

onion

tomato paste

all-purpose flour

kidney beans

green bell pepper

long-grain rice

chili powder

Worcestershire sauce

beef stock

chopped tomatoes

1 Heat the oil in a large pan and sauté the ground beef, onion and chili powder for 7 minutes.

2 Add the flour and tomato paste and cook for 1 minute. Stir in the stock and tomatoes and bring to a boil.

COOK'S TIP

This is a great meat dish to make for a party. You can easily just double or triple the ingredients. Cook one or two days ahead—the flavor will improve with keeping—then simply reheat thoroughly just before serving.

3 Add the kidney beans, green pepper and Worcestershire sauce and season with salt and pepper. Reduce the heat, simmer and continue to cook for about 45 minutes.

4 Meanwhile, cook the rice in boiling salted water for 10–12 minutes. Drain well. Spoon onto a serving plate. Spoon the chili over the rice, add a spoonful of sour cream and garnish with fresh parsley.

Coq au Vin

This classic French dish combines chicken, mushrooms, onions, bacon and herbs cooked in a rich red Burgundy.

Serves 4

INGREDIENTS

4 tablespoons all-purpose flour
3 pounds chicken, cut into 8 pieces
1 tablespoon olive oil
5 tablespoons butter
20 pearl onions
3-ounce slab of lean bacon without rind, diced
about 20 button mushrooms
2 tablespoons brandy
750 ml bottle red Burgundy
1 bouquet garni
3 garlic cloves
1 teaspoon light brown sugar
salt and freshly ground black pepper
1 tablespoon chopped fresh parsley and croutons, to garnish

flour

olive oil

chicken *butter*

bouquet garni

button mushrooms *brandy*

garlic

slab bacon

light brown sugar

pearl onions

red wine

1 Place 3 tablespoons of the flour and some seasoning in a large plastic bag and shake each chicken piece in it until lightly coated. Heat the oil and 4 tablespoons of the butter in a large flameproof casserole. Add the onions and bacon and sauté for 3–4 minutes, until the onions have browned lightly. Add the mushrooms and fry for 2 minutes. With a slotted spoon, transfer the onions, bacon and mushrooms to a bowl and reserve until needed.

2 Add the chicken pieces to the hot oil and cook until browned on all sides, 5–6 minutes. Pour in the brandy and (standing well back from the pan) carefully light it with a match, then shake the pan gently until the flames subside. Pour in the wine and add the bouquet garni, garlic, sugar and seasoning.

COOK'S TIP

If you would prefer not to tackle cutting up a whole chicken, buy 8 small ready-prepared chicken parts, such as thighs or drumsticks, or 4 larger wing or breast portions.

3 Bring to a boil, cover and simmer for 1 hour, stirring occasionally. Return the reserved onions, bacon and mushrooms to the casserole, cover and cook for 30 minutes more.

4 Lift out the chicken, vegetables and bacon with a slotted spoon and keep hot. Remove the bouquet garni and boil the liquid rapidly for 2 minutes. Cream the remaining butter and the flour together and whisk in teaspoonfuls of the mixture until the liquid has thickened slightly. Pour over the chicken and serve garnished with parsley and croutons.

Cassoulet

A traditional French dish, this recipe is full of delicious flavors and makes a warming meal.

Serves 6

INGREDIENTS
1 pound boneless duck breasts
8 ounces thick-cut lean salt pork or
    lean bacon strips
1 pound garlic sausages
3 tablespoons olive oil
1 pound onions, chopped
2 garlic cloves, crushed
2 cans (15 ounces each) cannellini
    beans, rinsed and drained
8 ounces carrots, roughly chopped
1 can (14 ounces) chopped tomatoes
1 tablespoon tomato paste
1 bouquet garni
2 tablespoons chopped fresh thyme
2 cups chicken stock
2 cups fresh bread crumbs
salt and freshly ground black pepper
fresh chopped thyme, to garnish

bacon

garlic
sausages

duck
breasts

carrot

onions

tomato
paste

olive oil

chopped
tomatoes

bread crumbs

thyme

bouquet
garni

garlic

chicken
stock

cannellini
beans

1 Preheat the oven to 325°F. Cut the duck breasts and salt pork or bacon slices into large pieces. Twist the sausages and cut into short lengths.

2 Heat the oil in a large flameproof casserole. Cook the meat in batches until well browned. Remove from the pan with a slotted spoon and drain on paper towels.

3 Add the onions and garlic to the pan and cook for 3–4 minutes, or until beginning to soften, stirring frequently.

4 Stir in the beans, carrots, tomatoes, tomato paste, bouquet garni, thyme and seasoning. Return the meat to the pan and mix until well combined.

5 Add enough of the stock just to cover the meat and beans. (The cassoulet shouldn't be swimming in juices; if the mixture becomes too dry, add a little more stock or water.) Bring to a boil. Cover tightly and cook in the oven for 1 hour.

COOK'S TIP

Garlic sausages are the classic ingredient for this meaty casserole, but any good-quality, flavorful, chunky, fresh sausages will do instead.

6 Remove the cassoulet from the oven, add a little more stock or water, if necessary, and remove the bouquet garni. Sprinkle the bread crumbs on top and return to the oven, uncovered, for another 40 minutes, or until the meat is tender and the top crisp. Brown under the broiler, if necessary, and garnish with fresh thyme.

Chicken Korma

Yogurt and cream give this sauce a rich flavor and contrast with the spicy chicken.

Serves 4

INGREDIENTS

1½ pounds chicken breasts, skinned and boned
2 tablespoons sunflower oil
1 ounce blanched almonds
2 garlic cloves, crushed
1-inch piece fresh ginger, roughly chopped
3 green cardamom pods
1 onion, finely chopped
2 teaspoons ground cumin
¼ teaspoon salt
⅔ cup plain yogurt
¾ cup light cream
toasted slivered almonds and a cilantro sprig, to garnish
boiled rice, to serve

chicken breasts

light cream

almonds

ground cumin

sunflower oil

fresh ginger

cardamom pods

plain yogurt

onion

garlic

1 Cut the skinned chicken breasts into 1-inch cubes.

2 Heat the oil in a large frying pan and cook the chicken for 8–10 minutes, or until browned. Meanwhile, put the almonds, garlic and ginger in a food processor or blender with 2 tablespoons water and process to a smooth paste. When the chicken is browned, remove from the pan with a slotted spoon and set aside.

3 Add the cardamom pods and fry for 2 minutes. Add the onion and fry for 5 minutes more.

4 Stir in the almond and garlic paste, cumin and salt and cook, stirring, for another 5 minutes.

5 Add the yogurt, a tablespoonful at a time, and cook over low heat until it has all been absorbed. Return the chicken to the pan. Cover and simmer over low heat for 5–6 minutes, or until the chicken is tender. Add the cream and simmer for another 5 minutes. Garnish with toasted slivered almonds and cilantro. Serve with boiled rice.

COOK'S TIP

Any leftover fresh ginger will keep for several weeks in the refrigerator. Wrap it in paper towels, place in an airtight container and store in the vegetable bin.

Rogan Josh

In this popular dish, the lamb is traditionally marinated in plain yogurt, then cooked with spices and tomatoes.

Serves 4

INGREDIENTS
2¼ pounds loin lamb fillet
3 tablespoons lemon juice
1 cup plain yogurt
1 teaspoon salt
2 garlic cloves, crushed
1-inch piece fresh ginger, grated
4 tablespoons sunflower oil
½ teaspoon cumin seeds
2 bay leaves
4 green cardamom pods
1 onion, finely chopped
2 teaspoons ground coriander
2 teaspoons ground cumin
1 teaspoon chili powder
1 can (14 ounces) chopped tomatoes
2 tablespoons tomato paste
toasted cumin seeds and bay leaves,
    to garnish
boiled rice, to serve

fresh ginger

sunflower oil

bay leaves

lamb fillet

ground cumin

ground coriander

chili powder

cumin seeds

chopped tomatoes *lemon juice* *plain yogurt* *cardamom pods* *garlic* *tomato paste* *onion*

1 Trim away any excess fat from the meat and cut into 1-inch cubes. Mix together the lemon juice, yogurt, salt, half the garlic and the ginger in a bowl. Add the lamb and let marinate in the refrigerator overnight.

2 Heat the oil in a large frying pan and fry the cumin seeds for 2 minutes, or until they begin to splutter. Add the bay leaves and cardamom pods and fry for another 2 minutes.

3 Add the onion and remaining garlic and fry for 5 minutes. Stir in the ground coriander, cumin and chili powder and fry for 2 minutes.

4 Add the marinated lamb and cook for 5 minutes, stirring occasionally.

COOK'S TIP

Don't omit the marinating process, as it both tenderizes the meat and improves the flavor. If you are short of time, marinate for only 1–2 hours.

5 Add the tomatoes, tomato paste and ⅔ cup water. Bring to a boil and reduce the heat. Cover and simmer for 1–1½ hours, or until the meat is tender. Garnish with toasted cumin seeds and bay leaves. Serve with boiled rice.

Calf's Liver with Onions

In this classic Venetian dish, the onions cook very slowly to produce a sweet flavor.

Serves 6

INGREDIENTS
6 tablespoons butter
3 tablespoons olive oil
1½ pounds onions, very finely sliced
1¾ pounds calf's liver, thinly sliced
salt and freshly ground black pepper
3 tablespoons finely chopped fresh
  parsley and sprigs, to garnish
grilled polenta wedges, to serve
  (optional)

olive oil

butter

calf's liver

onions

parsley

1 Heat two-thirds of the butter with the oil in a large, heavy frying pan. Add the onions and cook over low heat until soft and tender, 40–50 minutes, stirring often. Season with salt and pepper. Remove to a side dish.

2 Heat the remaining butter in the pan over moderate to high heat. When it has stopped bubbling, add the liver and brown it on both sides. Cook for about 5 minutes, or until done. Remove to a warmed side dish.

3 Return the onions to the pan. Raise the heat slightly, and stir the onions to mix them into the liver cooking juices.

4 When the onions are hot, turn them out onto a heated serving platter. Arrange the liver on top, and sprinkle with parsley. Serve with grilled polenta wedges, if desired.

COOK'S TIP
If you prefer, use thinly sliced lamb liver in place of the calf's liver.

Ground Meat Kebabs

In the Middle East, these kebabs traditionally are grilled but, if you prefer, they can also be cooked under a hot broiler.

Serves 6–8

INGREDIENTS
1 pound lean lamb
1 pound lean beef
1 large onion, grated
2 garlic cloves, crushed
1 tablespoon sumac (optional)
2 teaspoons baking soda
2–3 saffron strands, soaked in
    1 tablespoon boiling water
6–8 tomatoes, halved
1 tablespoon melted butter
salt and freshly ground black pepper
chopped fresh parsley, to garnish
boiled rice, to serve

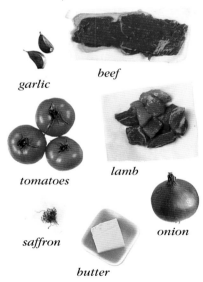

garlic

beef

tomatoes

lamb

saffron

onion

butter

COOK'S TIP
Sumac is a favorite Lebanese spice with a slightly sour but fruity flavor. It is available from most Middle Eastern food stores, but it is not essential in this recipe.

1 Grind the lamb and beef two or three times until very finely ground, place in a large bowl and add the grated onion, garlic, sumac, if using, baking soda, soaked saffron and salt and pepper.

2 Knead by hand for several minutes, until the mixture is very glutinous. It helps to have a bowl of water nearby in which to dip your fingers to keep the meat from sticking. Take several small handfuls of meat and roll them into balls.

3 Shape the balls around a flat skewer, molding them around the skewer. Repeat with three or four more balls on each skewer, pressing them tightly to prevent the meat from falling off.

4 Thread the tomatoes onto skewers and prepare a grill. Grill the kebabs for about 10 minutes, basting them with the melted butter and turning occasionally. Garnish with parsley and serve on a bed of rice.

Peppered Steaks with Madeira

An easy special-occasion dish—if you want to serve the steaks for a dinner party, you'll need to start marinating the steak either in the morning or the day before.

Serves 4

INGREDIENTS
1 tablespoon mixed dried peppercorns (green, pink and black)
4 sirloin steaks, about 6 ounces each
1 tablespoon extra virgin olive oil, plus extra for frying
1 garlic clove, crushed
4 tablespoons Madeira
6 tablespoons fresh beef stock
⅔ cup heavy cream
salt
salad and boiled potatoes, to serve

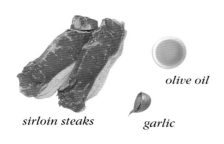

sirloin steaks   *garlic*   *olive oil*

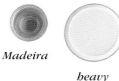

Madeira   *heavy cream*   *beef stock*

1 Finely crush the peppercorns using a mortar and pestle, then press onto both sides of the steaks.

2 Place the steaks in a shallow nonmetallic dish, then add the oil, garlic and Madeira. Cover and let marinate in a cool place for 4–6 hours, preferably overnight. Remove the steaks from the dish, reserving the marinade. Brush a little oil over a heavy frying pan and heat until hot.

3 Add the steaks and cook over high heat, allowing 3 minutes per side for medium or 2 minutes per side for rare. Remove and keep warm.

4 Add the reserved marinade and the stock to the pan and bring to a boil, then allow the sauce to bubble until it is well reduced. Add the cream, with salt to taste, to the pan and stir until slightly thickened. Serve the steaks with the sauce and salad and potatoes.

COOK'S TIP
Mixed green, pink and black peppercorns have an excellent flavor and add a pretty, speckled appearance to the steaks. However, if you can't find the mixed peppercorns, then use only one or two of the colors. Or simply use coarsely ground black pepper from a pepper mill instead.

Beef and Mushroom Burgers

The added mushrooms and bread crumbs give the burgers a robust flavor—and extra fiber.

Serves 4–5

INGREDIENTS
1 small onion, chopped
2 cups small button mushrooms
1 pound lean ground beef
1 cup fresh white or whole-wheat
    bread crumbs
1 teaspoon dried mixed herbs
1 tablespoon tomato paste
all-purpose flour, for shaping
salt and freshly ground black pepper
relish and salad greens,
    to garnish
soft hamburger buns or pita bread,
    to serve

mushrooms

tomato paste

ground beef

all-purpose flour

dried mixed herbs

onion

bread crumbs

1 Place the onion and mushrooms in a food processor or blender and process until finely chopped. Add the ground beef, white or whole-wheat bread crumbs, dried herbs and tomato paste. Season with plenty of salt and pepper. Process for a few seconds more, until the mixture binds together but still has a little texture.

4 Lift the burgers out of the pan and place in the buns or pita bread, with relish and salad greens to garnish.

2 Divide the mixture into eight to ten pieces, then press into burger shapes using lightly floured hands.

3 Cook the burgers in a nonstick frying pan or under a hot broiler for 12–15 minutes, turning once, until well browned and evenly cooked.

Cook's Tip

The mixture is quite soft, so handle it carefully and use a spatula for turning to prevent the burgers from breaking up during cooking. If you have time, chill the burgers for about half an hour before cooking to allow them to firm up slightly.

Beef Strips with Orange and Ginger

A quick and easy dish made with tender strips of beef and vegetables in a tangy sauce.

Serves 4

INGREDIENTS
1 pound lean beef rump, fillet or
    sirloin cut into thin strips
finely grated rind and juice of
    1 orange
1 tablespoon light soy sauce
1 teaspoon cornstarch
1-inch piece fresh ginger, finely
    chopped
2 teaspoons sesame oil
1 large carrot, cut into thin strips
2 scallions, thinly sliced
rice noodles or boiled rice,
    to serve

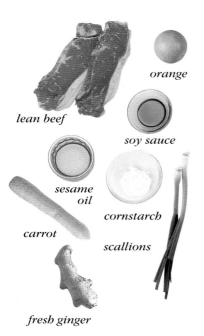

lean beef

orange

soy sauce

sesame oil

cornstarch

carrot

scallions

fresh ginger

1 Place the beef strips in a bowl and sprinkle the orange rind and juice over them. If possible, marinate for at least 30 minutes.

2 Drain the liquid from the meat and set aside, then mix the meat with the soy sauce, cornstarch and ginger.

3 Heat the oil in a wok or frying pan and add the beef. Stir-fry for 1 minute, until lightly colored, then add the carrot and stir-fry for 2–3 minutes.

4 Stir in the scallions and reserved liquid, then cook, stirring, until boiling and thickened. Serve hot with rice noodles or plain boiled rice.

VARIATION
This dish would be equally good with thin strips of lean lamb, chicken breast or turkey.

COOK'S TIP
It is important that the wok or frying pan be very hot before adding the marinated beef; otherwise, rather than frying and browning, it will tend to stew and not color.

Chicken Chow Mein

Chow mein is a classic Chinese noodle dish stir-fried with meat, seafood or vegetables.

Serves 4

INGREDIENTS

12 ounces Chinese egg noodles
8 ounces skinless, boneless chicken
    breasts
3 tablespoons soy sauce
1 tablespoon rice wine or dry sherry
1 tablespoon dark sesame oil
4 tablespoons sunflower oil
2 garlic cloves, finely chopped
2 ounces snow peas, trimmed
4 ounces (½ cup) bean sprouts
2 ounces ham, finely shredded
4 scallions, finely chopped
salt and freshly ground black pepper

egg noodles   *chicken breasts*   *ham*

soy sauce   *rice wine*   *sunflower oil*

snow peas

scallions

sesame oil

garlic

1 Cook the noodles in a saucepan of boiling water according to the package instructions until tender. Drain, rinse under cold water and drain well.

2 Slice the chicken into fine shreds about 2 inches in length. Place in a bowl and add 2 teaspoons of the soy sauce, the rice wine or sherry and the sesame oil.

3 Heat half the sunflower oil in a wok or large frying pan over high heat. When it starts smoking, add the chicken mixture. Stir-fry for 2 minutes, then transfer the chicken to a plate and keep it hot. Wipe the wok clean and heat the remaining oil. Stir in the garlic, snow peas, bean sprouts and ham, stir-fry for another minute or so and then add the cooked noodles.

4 Continue to stir-fry until the noodles are heated through. Add the remaining soy sauce to taste and season with salt and pepper. Return the chicken and any juices to the noodle mixture, add the chopped scallions and give the mixture a final stir. Serve immediately.

VARIATIONS

Lots of different ingredients can be used for this recipe. Try cooked, peeled shrimp, finely sliced beef or pork, sliced mushrooms, chopped baby corn or shredded bok choy in addition to or in place of some of the meat and vegetables.

COOK'S TIP

If you have time, slice the chicken ahead of time and let it marinate in the soy sauce mixture for up to 2 hours before cooking, to tenderize it.

Chinese Spiced Spareribs

Fragrant with spices, this authentic Chinese dish makes a great appetizer for an informal meal.

Serves 4

INGREDIENTS
1½–2¼ pounds meaty pork
    spareribs
1½ tablespoons cornstarch
peanut oil, for deep-frying
cilantro sprigs, to garnish

FOR THE SPICED SALT
1 teaspoon Szechuan peppercorns
2 tablespoons coarse sea salt
½ teaspoon Chinese five-spice
    powder

FOR THE MARINADE
2 tablespoons light soy sauce
1 teaspoon sugar
1 tablespoon Chinese rice wine
    or sherry
freshly ground black pepper

sea salt

pork
spareribs

soy sauce

cornstarch

rice
wine

peanut
oil

sugar

five-spice powder

Szechuan
peppercorns

1 Using a sharp, heavy cleaver, chop the spareribs into pieces about 2 inches long, or ask your butcher to do this. Place the ribs in a shallow dish.

3 Using a mortar and pestle or a clean electric coffee grinder, grind the spiced salt to a fine powder.

COOK'S TIP
Szechuan peppercorns have a lovely, aromatic flavor. They are available from supermarkets and Chinese food shops, but if you can't find them, use black peppercorns instead.

2 To make the spiced salt, heat a wok to medium. Add the Szechuan peppercorns and sea salt and dry-fry for about 3 minutes, stirring constantly, until the mixture colors slightly. Remove the wok from the heat and stir in the five-spice powder. Let cool.

4 Sprinkle 1 teaspoon of the spiced salt over the spareribs and rub in well with your hands. Place the soy sauce, sugar, rice wine or sherry and some freshly ground black pepper in a bowl, then toss the ribs in the marinade until well coated. Cover and let marinate in the refrigerator for about 2 hours, turning the spareribs occasionally.

5 Pour off any excess marinade from the spareribs. Sprinkle the pieces with cornstarch and mix well to coat evenly.

COOK'S TIP

Any leftover spiced salt can be kept for several months in a screw-top jar. Use to rub on the flesh of duck, chicken or pork before cooking.

6 Half-fill a wok with oil and heat to 350°F. Deep-fry the spareribs in batches for 3 minutes, until pale golden. Remove and set aside. Reheat the oil to the same temperature. Return the spareribs to the oil and deep-fry for a second time for 1–2 minutes, until crisp and cooked. Drain on paper towels. Transfer the ribs to a warmed platter and sprinkle 1–1½ teaspoons of the spiced salt over them. Garnish with cilantro sprigs and serve immediately.

Chicken Kiev with Ricotta

Cut through the crisp-coated chicken to reveal a creamy filling with just a hint of garlic.

Serves 4

INGREDIENTS
4 large chicken breasts, boned
 and skinned
1 tablespoon lemon juice
½ cup ricotta cheese
1 garlic clove, crushed
2 tablespoons chopped fresh parsley
¼ teaspoon freshly grated nutmeg
2 tablespoons all-purpose flour
pinch of cayenne pepper
¼ teaspoon salt
2 cups fresh white bread crumbs
2 egg whites, lightly beaten
parsley sprigs, to garnish
duchess potatoes, green beans and
 broiled tomatoes, to serve

chicken breasts

bread crumbs

ricotta cheese *garlic*

lemon juice

eggs

parsley

all-purpose flour

1 Preheat the oven to 400°F. Place the chicken breasts between two sheets of plastic wrap and gently beat with a rolling pin until flattened. Sprinkle with the lemon juice.

2 Mix the ricotta cheese with the garlic, 1 tablespoon of the chopped parsley, and the nutmeg. Shape into four 2-inch-long cylinders.

3 Put one portion of the cheese and herb mixture in the center of each chicken breast and fold the meat over, tucking in all the edges to enclose the filling completely.

4 Secure the chicken with toothpicks pushed through the center of each roll. Mix together the flour, cayenne pepper and salt. Dust the chicken with the seasoned flour.

5 Mix together the bread crumbs and remaining parsley. Dip the chicken into the egg whites, then coat with the bread crumbs. Chill for 30 minutes in the refrigerator, then dip into the egg white and bread crumbs for a second time.

6 Put the chicken on a nonstick baking sheet and spray with nonstick cooking spray. Bake in the preheated oven for 25 minutes, or until the coating is golden brown and the chicken is completely cooked. Remove the toothpicks and garnish with parsley. Serve with duchess potatoes, green beans and broiled tomatoes.

Roast Chicken with Lemon and Herbs

Use a flavorful chicken for this classic dish—free-range would be ideal.

Serves 4

INGREDIENTS
3-pound chicken
1 unwaxed lemon, halved
small bunch thyme sprigs
1–2 bay leaves
1 tablespoon butter, softened
4–6 tablespoons chicken stock or
    water
salt and freshly ground black pepper

chicken

butter   *bay leaves*

thyme

chicken stock

lemon

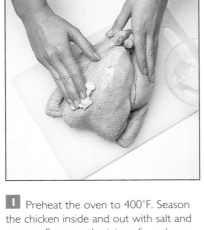

1 Preheat the oven to 400°F. Season the chicken inside and out with salt and pepper. Squeeze the juice of one lemon half and then place the juice, the squeezed lemon half, the thyme and the bay leaves in the chicken cavity. Tie the legs with string and rub the breast with butter.

COOK'S TIP
Be sure to save the carcasses of roast poultry for stock. Freeze them until you have several, then simmer with aromatic vegetables, herbs and water.

2 Place the chicken on a rack in a roasting pan. Squeeze the juice of the other lemon half over it. Roast for 1 hour, basting two or three times, until the juices run clear when the thickest part of the thigh is pierced with a knife.

3 Pour the juices from the cavity into the roasting pan and transfer the chicken to a carving board. Cover loosely with foil and let stand for 10–15 minutes before carving.

4 Skim off the fat from the cooking juices. Add the stock or water and boil over medium heat, stirring and scraping the bottom of the pan, until slightly reduced. Strain and serve with the roast chicken.

Roast Rabbit with Three Mustards

Each of the three different mustards in this recipe adds a distinctive flavor to the dish.

Serves 4

INGREDIENTS
1 tablespoon Dijon mustard
1 tablespoon tarragon mustard
1 tablespoon whole-grain mustard
3–3½ pounds rabbit pieces
1 large carrot, sliced
1 onion, sliced
2 tablespoons chopped fresh
    tarragon
½ cup dry white wine
⅔ cup heavy cream
salt and freshly ground black pepper
fresh tarragon, to garnish

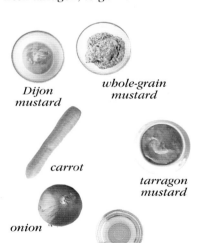

Dijon mustard   *whole-grain mustard*

carrot

tarragon mustard

onion

dry white wine

heavy cream   *tarragon*

rabbit pieces

VARIATION

If the three different mustards are not available, use one or two varieties, increasing the quantities accordingly. The flavor will not be quite as interesting, but the dish will still taste good.

1 Preheat the oven to 400°F. Mix the mustards in a bowl, then spread the mixture evenly over the rabbit pieces.

2 Put the carrot and onion slices in a large roasting pan and scatter the chopped tarragon over the top. Pour in ½ cup water, then arrange the meat on top.

3 Roast for 25–30 minutes, basting frequently with the juices, until the rabbit is tender. Remove the rabbit to a heated serving dish and keep hot. Using a slotted spoon, carefully remove the carrot and onion slices from the roasting pan and discard.

4 Place the roasting pan on the stove and add the white wine. Boil to reduce by about two-thirds. Stir in the heavy cream and allow to bubble up for a few minutes. Season with salt and pepper and pour over the rabbit. Serve garnished with fresh tarragon.

Roast Turkey

Everyone needs a foolproof recipe for the traditional Thanksgiving turkey, stuffing and gravy.

Serves 4

INGREDIENTS

10-pound oven-ready turkey, with
  giblets (defrosted if frozen)
1 large onion, peeled, halved and
  stuck with 6 whole cloves
4 tablespoons butter, softened
10 breakfast sausages
salt and freshly ground black pepper
mixed fresh herbs, to garnish
mixed vegetables, to serve

FOR THE STUFFING

8 ounces rindless lean
  bacon, chopped
1 large onion, finely chopped
1 pound pork sausage meat
⅓ cup rolled oats
2 tablespoons chopped fresh parsley
2 teaspoons mixed dried herbs
1 large egg, beaten
4 ounces dried apricots,
  finely chopped

FOR THE GRAVY

2 tablespoons all-purpose flour
2 cups giblet stock

turkey

butter   *egg*

rolled oats

fresh parsley

sausage meat

onion

dried apricots

lean bacon   *breakfast sausages*

1 Preheat the oven to 400°F. To make the stuffing, cook the bacon and onion gently in a pan until the bacon is crisp and the onion is tender. Transfer to a large bowl and mix in all the remaining stuffing ingredients. Season with salt and pepper.

2 Stuff the neck end of the turkey only, tuck the flap of skin under and secure it with a small skewer or stitch it with thread (do not overstuff the turkey, or the skin will burst during cooking). Reserve any remaining stuffing.

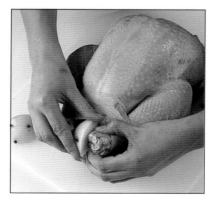

3 Put the onion halves studded with cloves in the body cavity of the turkey and tie the legs together. Taking the weight of the stuffing into account, calculate the cooking time: Allow 15 minutes per pound plus 15 minutes. Place the turkey in a large roasting pan.

4 Spread the turkey with butter and season with salt and pepper. Cover it loosely with foil and cook for 30 minutes. Baste the turkey with the pan juices, then lower the oven temperature to 350°F and cook for the remainder of the calculated time (about 3½ hours for a 10-pound bird). Baste it every 30 minutes or so.

5 With wet hands, shape the remaining stuffing into small balls, place in a small roasting dish with the sausages and set aside. Remove the foil from the turkey for the last hour of cooking and baste it. About 5 minutes before the end of cooking, put the stuffing balls and sausages in the oven and cook for 20 minutes, or until golden brown.

COOK'S TIP

Before you turn on the oven, adjust the oven shelves to allow for the size of the turkey.

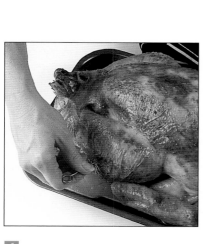

6 The turkey is cooked if the juices run clear when the thickest part of the thigh has been pierced with a skewer. Transfer the turkey to a serving plate, cover with foil and let it stand for about 15 minutes before carving. To make the gravy, spoon off the fat from the pan, leaving the meat juices. Blend in the flour and cook for 2 minutes. Stir in the stock and bring to a boil. Check the seasoning and pour into a gravy boat. Remove the skewer or string and pour any juices into the gravy. Garnish the turkey with fresh herbs and serve it with sausages, bacon rolls, stuffing balls and mixed vegetables.

Mediterranean Chicken

This is the perfect supper-party dish—quick to prepare and full of sunshiny flavors.

Serves 4

INGREDIENTS

4 chicken breasts and wing portions,
    about 1½ pounds total weight
4 ounces (1 cup) soft cheese with
    garlic and herbs
1 pound zucchini
2 red bell peppers, seeded
1 pound plum tomatoes
4 celery stalks
about 2 tablespoons olive oil
10 ounces onions, roughly chopped
3 garlic cloves, crushed
8 sun-dried tomatoes, roughly
    chopped
1 teaspoon dried oregano
2 tablespoons balsamic vinegar
salt and 1 teaspoon paprika
olive ciabatta or crusty bread,
    to serve

chicken breasts

zucchini

bell peppers

sun-dried tomatoes

balsamic vinegar

celery

garlic cloves

onions

plum tomatoes

olive oil

dried oregano

soft cheese

1 Preheat the oven to 375°F. Loosen the skin of each chicken, without removing it, to make a pocket. Push one-quarter of the cheese underneath the skin of each chicken breast in an even layer.

2 Cut the zucchini and peppers into similar-size chunks. Quarter the tomatoes and slice the celery stalks.

3 Heat 2 tablespoons of the oil in a large, shallow flameproof casserole. Cook the onions and garlic for 4 minutes, until they are soft and golden, stirring them frequently.

4 Add the zucchini, peppers and celery and cook for another 5 minutes.

5 Stir in the tomatoes, sun-dried tomatoes, oregano and balsamic vinegar. Season well.

6 Place the chicken on top, drizzle with a little more olive oil and season with salt and paprika. Bake for 35–40 minutes, or until the chicken is golden and cooked through. Serve with plenty of olive ciabatta or crusty bread.

Roast Duck with Orange

Already a popular alternative on the festive feast menu, duck and oranges make the perfect combination here.

Serves 8

INGREDIENTS
4 oranges, segmented, with rind and
    juice reserved
2 x 5-pound oven-ready ducks, with
    giblets
salt and freshly ground black pepper
fresh parsley sprig, to garnish

FOR THE SAUCE
2 tablespoons all-purpose flour
1¼ cups chicken or duck stock
⅔ cup port or red wine
1 tablespoon red currant jelly

chicken stock

ducks

port

oranges

all-purpose flour

red currant jelly

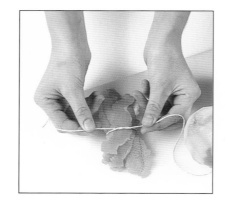

1 Preheat the oven to 350°F. Tie the orange rind with string and place it inside the cavities of the two ducks.

2 Place the ducks on a rack in one large or two smaller pans, prick the skin well, season well and cook for 30 minutes per pound (about 2½ hours), until the flesh is tender and the juices run clear. Carefully pour off the fat from the roasting pan(s) into a bowl halfway through the cooking time. Transfer the ducks to a carving board and remove the orange rind from the cavities.

3 To make the sauce, remove any fat from the roasting pan, leaving the sediment and juices behind. Sprinkle in the flour and cook gently for 2 minutes. Blend in the rest of the ingredients and reserved orange rind, roughly chopped. Bring to a boil and simmer for about 10 minutes, then strain into a pan. Add the orange segments with their juices.

4 To carve the ducks, remove the legs and wings, cutting through the joints. Cut the two end joints off the wings and discard them. Cut the breast meat off the carcass in one piece and slice it thinly. Arrange the slices on a warmed serving plate with the legs and the wing joints. Spoon some of the hot sauce on top and serve the rest separately, in a sauceboat. Garnish with parsley and serve.

Roast Pheasant with Port

This recipe is best for very young pheasants; female birds are the most tender.

Serves 4

INGREDIENTS

2 oven-ready pheasants, about 1½
   pounds each
4 tablespoons unsalted butter,
   softened
8 thyme sprigs
2 bay leaves
6 bacon strips
1 tablespoon all-purpose flour
¾ cup game or chicken stock, plus
   more if needed
1 tablespoon red currant jelly
3–4 tablespoons port
freshly ground black pepper
fresh thyme sprigs and bay leaves,
   to garnish

bay leaves

butter

thyme

pheasants

game stock

port

red currant jelly

bacon

1 Preheat the oven to 450°F. Line a roasting pan with a sheet of foil large enough to enclose the pheasants. Brush the foil with oil. Wipe the pheasants with damp paper towels and remove extra fat or skin. Using your fingertips, loosen the breast skin. With a round-bladed knife, spread the butter between the skin and breast meat. Tie the legs securely, then lay the thyme and bay leaves over each breast.

2 Lay bacon strips over the breasts, place the birds in the foil-lined pan and season with pepper. Bring together the long ends of the foil, fold over securely to enclose, then seal the ends.

3 Roast the birds for 20 minutes, then reduce the oven temperature to 375°F and cook for another 40 minutes. Uncover the birds and roast for 10–15 minutes more, or until they are browned and the juices run clear when the thigh of a bird is pierced with a knife. Transfer the birds to a board and let stand, covered with clean foil, for 10 minutes before carving.

4 Carefully pour the juices from the foil into the roasting pan and skim off any fat. Sprinkle in the flour and cook over medium heat, stirring until smooth. Whisk in the stock and bring to a boil, stirring constantly.

5 Add the red currant jelly and bring to a boil. Simmer until the sauce thickens slightly, adding more stock if needed. Stir in the port and season. Strain and serve with the pheasant, garnished with herbs.

Beef Wellington with Mushrooms

Traditionally this dish calls for goose liver pâté, but mushroom pâté is cheaper and tastes equally delicious.

Serves 4

INGREDIENTS

1½-pound beef tenderloin, tied
1 tablespoon sunflower oil
12 ounces puff pastry, defrosted
    if frozen
1 egg, beaten, to glaze
salt and freshly ground black pepper

FOR THE PARSLEY PANCAKES
4 tablespoons all-purpose flour
⅔ cup milk
1 egg
2 tablespoons chopped fresh parsley

FOR THE MUSHROOM PÂTÉ
2 shallots or 1 small onion, chopped
2 tablespoons unsalted butter
1 pound assorted wild and
    cultivated mushrooms, such as
    oyster mushrooms, cèpes or
    chanterelles, trimmed and
    chopped
1 cup fresh white bread crumbs,
    combined with 5 tablespoons
    heavy cream and 2 egg yolks

sunflower oil

eggs

shallots

heavy cream

wild mushrooms

puff pastry

bread crumbs

butter

milk

all-purpose flour

1 Preheat the oven to 425°F. Season the beef with several grindings of black pepper. Heat the oil in a roasting pan, add the beef and quickly sear to brown all sides. Transfer to the preheated oven and roast for 15 minutes for rare, 20 minutes for medium-rare or 25 minutes for well-done meat. Set aside to cool. Reduce the temperature to 375°F.

2 To make the pancakes, beat the flour, a pinch of salt, half the milk, the egg and the parsley together until smooth, then stir in the remaining milk. Heat a greased nonstick pan and pour in enough batter to coat the bottom. When set, turn over and cook the other side briefly until lightly browned. Continue with remaining batter—the recipe makes three or four.

3 To make the pâté, fry the shallots in butter to soften without coloring. Add the mushrooms and cook until the juices begin to run. Increase the heat and cook briskly until the juices evaporate completely. Add the bread crumb and cream mixture and blend to make a smooth paste. Allow to cool.

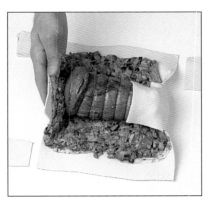

4 Roll out the pastry and cut to a 14 x 12-inch rectangle. Arrange the pancakes on the pastry and spread with pâté. Place the beef on top and spread over any remaining pâté. Cut four squares from the corners of the pastry. Moisten the edges with egg and wrap them over the meat.

COOK'S TIP

Instead of using a meat thermometer, you can insert a metal skewer into the meat. If the skewer is cold, the meat is not done, if it is warm, the meat is rare and if it is hot, it is well done.

5 Decorate the top with the reserved pastry trimmings, transfer to a baking sheet and let rest in a cool place until ready to cook.

6 Brush evenly with beaten egg. Cook the Wellington for about 40 minutes, until golden brown. To ensure that the meat is heated through, test with a meat thermometer. It should read 125–130°F for rare, 135°F for medium-rare and 160°F for well-done meat.

Baked Ham with Cumberland Sauce

Serve this delicious cooked meat and tangy sauce either hot or cold.

Serves 8–10

INGREDIENTS
5-pound smoked or unsmoked ham
1 onion
1 carrot
1 celery stalk
1 bouquet garni
6 peppercorns
whole cloves
4 tablespoons light brown
  or demerara sugar
2 tablespoons golden syrup or light
  corn syrup
1 teaspoon English mustard powder

FOR THE CUMBERLAND SAUCE
shredded rind and juice of 1 orange
2 tablespoons lemon juice
½ cup port or red wine
4 tablespoons red currant jelly

ham · cloves · onion · port · orange · carrot · lemon · golden syrup · red currant jelly · light brown sugar · celery · bouquet garni · peppercorns · mustard powder

COOK'S TIP

To serve the ham cold, loosely cover it and leave it in a cool place until completely cool, then wrap more tightly in foil and transfer to the refrigerator until ready to carve.

1 Soak the ham overnight in a cool place in plenty of cold water to cover. Discard this water. Put the ham in a large pan and cover it again with more cold water. Bring the water to a boil slowly and skim off any scum from the surface with a slotted spoon.

2 Cut the vegetables into chunks and add to the pan with the bouquet garni and peppercorns. Cover and simmer very gently for 2 hours. (The meat can also be cooked in the oven at 350°F. Allow 30 minutes per pound.)

3 Let the meat cool in the liquid for 30 minutes. Then remove it from the liquid and strip off the skin neatly with the help of a knife (use rubber gloves if the ham is too hot to handle).

4 Score the fat in diamonds with a sharp knife and stick a clove in the center of each diamond.

5 Preheat the oven to 350°F. Put the sugar, syrup and mustard powder in a small pan and heat gently to melt. Place the ham in a roasting pan and spoon the glaze over it. Bake for about 20 minutes, until golden brown. Put the ham under a hot broiler, if necessary, to get a good color. Let stand in a warm place for 15 minutes before carving (to allow the flesh to relax and make carving easier).

6 To make the sauce, put the orange and lemon juice into a pan with the port and red currant jelly, and heat gently to melt the jelly. Pour boiling water onto the orange rind, drain, and add to the sauce. Cook gently for 2 minutes. Serve the sauce hot, in a sauceboat.

Pot-Roasted Glazed Lamb

The vegetables in this pot roast turn tender and caramelized, full of the flavors of the meat.

Serves 6

INGREDIENTS
12 garlic cloves
2½-pound leg of lamb
   (knuckle end)
about 12 small fresh rosemary sprigs
3 tablespoons olive oil
12 shallots, peeled
2 pounds potatoes, cut into chunks
1½ pounds parsnips, cut into
   large chunks
1½ pounds carrots, cut into chunks
1¼ cups red wine
3 tablespoons honey
2 tablespoons dark soy sauce
2 teaspoons all-purpose flour
2 cups lamb stock
salt and freshly ground black pepper
fresh rosemary sprigs, to garnish

soy sauce honey rosemary
garlic red wine
leg of lamb all-purpose flour
shallots lamb stock carrots
potatoes olive oil parsnips

1 Preheat the oven to 375°F. Peel three of the cloves of garlic and slice. Make slits all over the meat and insert slices of garlic and small sprigs of rosemary. Season well.

2 Heat the oil in a large flameproof casserole or roasting pan and add the shallots. Cook, stirring occasionally, until they begin to turn golden.

3 Add the potatoes, parsnips, carrots and remaining garlic cloves. Stir to coat the vegetables in the oil. Season. Place the lamb on top and pour half the red wine over it. Cover tightly, place in the oven and cook for 1 hour. Baste occasionally with any fat and juices.

4 Mix together the honey and soy sauce until combined. After the first hour of cooking, pour the honey mixture over the lamb and baste. Return to the oven, uncovered, for another 1–1¼ hours, basting the meat and vegetables from time to time.

5 Test that the meat is cooked and the vegetables are tender. Remove from the pan and let the meat rest for 10–15 minutes before carving (keep the vegetables warm).

6 Place the casserole or roasting pan on the stove, stir in the flour and cook for 1 minute. Blend in the stock and remaining wine, then bring to a boil and adjust the seasoning. Serve the meat and vegetables with plenty of the sauce spooned over them, garnished with fresh rosemary sprigs.

Roast Beef with Yorkshire Puddings

The classic British Sunday lunchtime meal reminds us why it's worth keeping this tasty tradition alive.

Serves 6

INGREDIENTS
4-pound rib roast, either on the
    bone or boned and rolled
2–4 tablespoons sunflower oil
1¼ cups beef stock, wine or water
salt and freshly ground black pepper

FOR THE YORKSHIRE PUDDINGS
½ cup all-purpose flour
1 egg, beaten
⅔ cup mixed water and milk
sunflower oil, for cooking

1 Calculate the cooking time for the beef, allowing 15 minutes per pound plus 15 minutes for rare, 20 minutes plus 20 minutes for medium and 25–30 minutes plus 25 minutes for well-done meat.

2 Preheat the oven to 425°F. Heat the sunflower oil in a roasting pan in the oven.

3 Place the beef on a rack, fat side on the top, then place the rack in the roasting pan. Baste the beef with the oil and cook as required, basting occasionally.

rib roast

sunflower oil

all-purpose flour

beef stock

egg

6 Spoon off the fat from the roasting pan. Add the stock, wine or water, stirring to dislodge the sediment, and boil for a few minutes. Check the seasoning, then serve with the beef and the Yorkshire puddings.

COOK'S TIP
To achieve light and crisp Yorkshire puddings, make sure that the muffin cups of oil are very hot before adding the batter, then return the pan to the oven immediately—don't allow it to cool. Cook in the top third of the oven for the best results.

4 To make the Yorkshire puddings, stir the flour and salt and pepper together in a bowl and form a well in the center. Pour the egg into the well, then slowly pour in the water and milk, stirring in the flour to make a smooth batter. Let stand for 30 minutes.

5 A few minutes before the meat is ready, pour a little oil into each cup of a 12-cup muffin pan and place in the oven until very hot. Remove the meat from the oven, season, then cover loosely with foil and keep warm. Quickly divide the batter among the cups, then bake for 15–20 minutes, until well risen and golden brown.

Sausage and Red Onion Pizza

You could substitute fresh hot Italian sausages in this recipe—they are available at large supermarkets and at good Italian delicatessens.

Serves 3–4

INGREDIENTS

8 ounces good-quality pork sausages
1 teaspoon mild chili powder
½ teaspoon freshly ground
  black pepper
2 tablespoons olive oil
2–3 garlic cloves
1 ready-made pizza crust,
  10–12 inches in diameter
⅔ cup chunky tomato sauce
1 red onion, thinly sliced
1 tablespoon chopped
  fresh oregano
1 tablespoon chopped fresh thyme
2 ounces mozzarella cheese, grated
2 ounces Parmesan cheese,
  freshly grated

oregano and thyme

tomato sauce

mozzarella cheese

red onion

Parmesan cheese

olive oil

pork sausages

garlic

chili powder

1 Preheat the oven to 425°F. Skin the sausages by running a sharp knife down the side of the skins. Place the sausage meat in a bowl and add the chili powder and black pepper; mix well. Break the sausage meat into walnut-size balls.

2 Heat 1 tablespoon of the oil in a frying pan and fry the sausage balls for 2–3 minutes, until evenly browned.

3 Using a slotted spoon, remove the sausage balls from the pan and drain on paper towels.

4 Cut the garlic cloves into thin slices using a small sharp knife.

5 Brush the pizza crust with the remaining oil, then spread with the tomato sauce. Scatter the sausages, garlic, onion and herbs on top.

6 Sprinkle with the mozzarella and Parmesan and bake for 15–20 minutes, until crisp and golden. Serve immediately.

Pepperoni Pizza

This popular pizza is spiced with green chiles and pepperoni.

Serves 2–3

INGREDIENTS
1 ready-made pizza crust,
    10–12 inches in diameter
1 tablespoon olive oil
1 can (4 ounces) peeled and chopped
    green chiles, drained
⅔ cup chunky tomato sauce
¾ cup sliced pepperoni
6 pitted black olives
1 tablespoon chopped
    fresh oregano
4 ounces mozzarella cheese, grated
oregano leaves, to garnish

mozzarella cheese

oregano   *tomato sauce*

pepperoni

olive oil

chopped green chiles   *black olives*

1 Preheat the oven to 425°F. Place the pizza crust on a baking sheet and brush evenly all over the top with the oil.

2 Stir the chopped chiles into the tomato sauce, then spread the sauce over the pizza, leaving about 1 inch around the edge clear.

3 Sprinkle the sliced pepperoni over the sauce.

4 Halve the olives lengthwise and sprinkle them over the sauce with the fresh oregano.

5 Sprinkle the grated mozzarella over the top and bake for 15–20 minutes, until the pizza is crisp and golden.

6 Garnish the pizza with oregano leaves and serve immediately.

VARIATION

You can make this pizza as hot as you like. For a really fiery version, use fresh red or green chiles, cut into thin slices, in place of the canned chiles.

Spaghetti Carbonara

It is said that this dish was originally cooked by Italian coal miners—or charcoal burners—hence the name "carbonara."

Serves 4

INGREDIENTS
6 ounces pancetta (unsmoked Italian bacon) or bacon
1 garlic clove, chopped
3 eggs
1 pound spaghetti
4 tablespoons grated Parmesan
salt and freshly ground black pepper
fresh parsley sprigs, to garnish

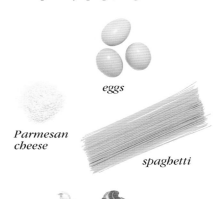

eggs

Parmesan cheese

spaghetti

garlic

bacon

parsley

COOK'S TIP
Be careful not to overcook the egg if you want to achieve a creamy sauce.

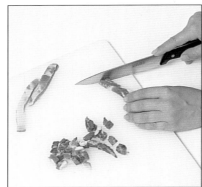

1 Cut the pancetta or bacon into dice and place in a saucepan. Set over the heat and fry in its own fat with the garlic until brown. Keep warm until needed.

2 Put the eggs in a bowl and whisk together lightly.

3 Cook the spaghetti in a large saucepan of boiling salted water for 10–12 minutes, or according to the package instructions, until al dente. Drain well.

4 Quickly turn the spaghetti into the pan with the pancetta and stir in the eggs, a little salt, lots of pepper and half the cheese. Toss well to mix. The eggs should just half cook with the heat from the spaghetti. Serve with the remaining cheese and garnish with fresh parsley.

Tagliatelle with Bolognese Sauce

Tagliatelle is the traditional pasta for Bolognese sauce, the famous *ragù* from Bologna.

Serves 4

INGREDIENTS
12 ounces dried tagliatelle
shredded fresh basil, to garnish
grated Parmesan cheese, to serve

FOR THE BOLOGNESE SAUCE
2 tablespoons olive oil
1 onion, finely chopped
1 carrot, finely chopped
1 celery stalk, finely chopped
1 garlic clove, crushed
12 ounces (2½ cups) ground beef
⅔ cup red wine
1 cup milk
1 can (14 ounces) chopped tomatoes
1 tablespoon sun-dried tomato paste
salt and freshly ground black pepper

basil
garlic
onion
carrot
olive oil
ground beef
red wine
chopped tomatoes
milk
tomato paste
celery

COOK'S TIP
Don't skimp on the cooking time—it is essential for a full-flavored Bolognese sauce. Some Italian cooks insist on cooking it for 3–4 hours, so the longer the better.

1 To make the Bolognese sauce, heat the oil in a large saucepan. Add the onion, carrot, celery and garlic and cook gently, stirring frequently, for about 10 minutes, until softened. Do not allow the vegetables to color.

2 Add the ground beef to the pan with the vegetables and cook over medium heat until the meat changes color, stirring constantly and breaking up any lumps with a wooden spoon.

3 Pour in the wine. Stir frequently until it has evaporated, then add the milk and continue cooking and stirring until it has evaporated too.

4 Stir in the tomatoes, tomato paste and salt and pepper. Simmer gently, uncovered, for 45 minutes. Cook the tagliatelle in boiling salted water for 8–10 minutes, or until al dente. Drain, add the sauce and toss to combine. Garnish with basil and serve with Parmesan.

Lasagne

This lasagne, made from egg pasta with homemade Bolognese and béchamel sauces, is truly exquisite.

Serves 8–10

INGREDIENTS
1 recipe Bolognese sauce (see page 83)
14 ounces fresh or dried lasagne
1 cup grated Parmesan cheese
3 tablespoons butter

FOR THE BÉCHAMEL SAUCE
3 cups milk
1–2 bay leaves
3 blades mace
½ cup butter
¾ cup all-purpose flour
salt and freshly ground black pepper

Bolognese sauce   *butter*   *milk*

bay leaves

all-purpose flour

Parmesan cheese   *lasagne*

VARIATION
If you are using dried bought pasta, follow step 4, but boil the lasagne in just two batches, and stop the cooking 4 minutes before the recommended cooking time on the package has elapsed. Rinse in cold water and lay the pasta out the same way as for egg pasta.

1 Prepare the Bolognese sauce, then set aside. Butter a large shallow baking dish, preferably rectangular or square.

2 Make the béchamel sauce by gently heating the milk with the bay leaves and mace in a small saucepan. Melt the butter in a saucepan. Add the flour, and mix it in well with a wire whisk. Cook for 2–3 minutes.

3 Strain the hot milk into the flour and butter, and mix smoothly with the whisk. Bring the sauce to a boil, stirring constantly, and cook for 4–5 minutes more. Season with salt and pepper, and set aside.

4 If using homemade fresh pasta, cut it into rectangles about 4½ inches wide and the same length as the baking dish (this will make it easier to assemble). Preheat the oven to 400°F.

5 Bring a large pan of salted water to a boil. Place a bowl of cold water near the stove. Drop in several of the pasta rectangles. Cook briefly, about 30 seconds. Remove from the pan and drop into the bowl of cold water for about 30 seconds. Pull them out, shaking off the excess water. Lay them on a dish towel. Continue with the rest of the pasta.

6 To assemble the lasagne, have all the elements at hand: the baking dish, béchamel and meat sauces, pasta strips, grated Parmesan cheese and butter. Spread one large spoonful of the meat sauce over the bottom of the dish. Add a thin layer of béchamel sauce, then arrange a layer of pasta in the dish, cutting it with a sharp knife so that it fits well inside the dish.

7 Cover with a thin layer of meat sauce, then one of béchamel. Sprinkle with a little cheese. Repeat the layers in the same order, ending with a layer of pasta coated with béchamel. Sprinkle the top with Parmesan, and dot with butter. Bake for 20 minutes, or until brown on top. Remove from the oven and let stand for 5 minutes before serving. Serve directly from the baking dish.

Cannelloni with Chicken and Mushrooms

Using chicken makes a lighter alternative to the usual beef-filled, béchamel-coated version.

Serves 4–6

INGREDIENTS
1 pound skinless, boneless chicken
    breasts, cooked
8 ounces mushrooms
2 garlic cloves, crushed
2 tablespoons chopped fresh parsley
1 tablespoon chopped fresh
    tarragon
1 egg, beaten
fresh lemon juice
12–18 cannelloni tubes
1¼ cups tomato sauce
½ cup freshly grated Parmesan
    cheese
salt and freshly ground black pepper
sprig of fresh parsley, to garnish

egg *garlic*

mushrooms *cooked chicken breasts*

lemon

cannelloni *tomato sauce*

parsley

Parmesan cheese

tarragon

1 Preheat the oven to 400°F. Place the chicken in a food processor or blender and process until finely minced. Transfer to a bowl.

2 Place the mushrooms, garlic, parsley and tarragon in the food processor or blender and process until finely minced.

3 Beat the mushroom mixture into the chicken with the egg, salt and pepper and lemon juice to taste.

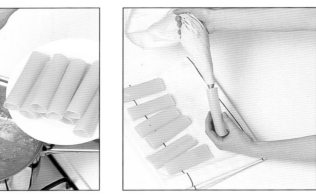

4 Cook the cannelloni in plenty of salted boiling water according to the manufacturer's instructions. Drain well on a clean dish towel.

5 Place the filling in a pastry bag fitted with a large plain nozzle. Use this to fill each tube of cannelloni.

6 Lay the filled cannelloni tightly together in a single layer in a buttered shallow ovenproof dish. Spoon the tomato sauce over them and sprinkle with Parmesan cheese. Bake for 30 minutes, or until brown and bubbling. Serve garnished with a sprig of parsley.

Pastitsio

This simple Greek dish combines pasta, lamb and yogurt in a delicious casserole.

Serves 4

INGREDIENTS
1 tablespoon olive oil
4 cups ground lamb
1 onion, chopped
2 garlic cloves, crushed
2 tablespoons tomato paste
2 tablespoons all-purpose flour
1¼ cups lamb stock
2 large tomatoes
1 cup pasta shapes
16 ounces plain yogurt
2 eggs
salt and freshly ground black pepper
mixed salad and crusty bread,
    to serve

olive oil   *ground lamb*

garlic   *onion*

tomato paste

plain yogurt   *all-purpose flour*

tomatoes

eggs

lamb stock

pasta shapes

1 Heat the oil in a large pan and fry the lamb for 5 minutes. Add the onion and garlic and continue to fry for another 5 minutes.

2 Stir in the tomato paste and flour. Cook for 1 minute. Stir in the stock and season to taste. Bring to a boil and cook for 20 minutes. Preheat the oven to 375°F.

3 Slice the tomatoes, place the meat in an ovenproof dish and arrange the tomatoes on top.

4 Cook the pasta in plenty of rapidly boiling salted water for 8–10 minutes, or until al dente. Drain thoroughly and mix with the yogurt and eggs. Spoon the pasta mixture on top of the tomatoes and bake for about 1 hour, until golden brown and bubbling. Serve hot with a mixed salad and some crusty bread.

VARIATION
Use ground beef instead of the lamb, if you prefer.

Shepherd's Pie

This warming supper dish is an all-time favorite, especially with children.

Serves 4

INGREDIENTS

2 tablespoons sunflower oil
1 onion, finely chopped
1 carrot, finely chopped
4 ounces mushrooms, chopped
1¼ pounds lean ground lamb
1¼ cups lamb stock or water
1 tablespoon all-purpose flour
1–2 bay leaves
2–3 teaspoons Worcestershire sauce
1 tablespoon tomato paste
1½ pounds potatoes, boiled
2 tablespoons butter
3 tablespoons hot milk
1 tablespoon chopped
    fresh tarragon
salt and freshly ground black pepper
fresh tarragon sprig, to garnish

milk
carrot
mushrooms
onion
tomato paste
butter
all-purpose flour
Worcestershire sauce
sunflower oil
bay leaves
ground lamb
lamb stock
potatoes
tarragon

1 Heat the oil in a pan, add the onion, carrot and mushrooms and cook, stirring occasionally, until browned. Add the lamb and cook, stirring to break up the lumps, until lightly browned.

2 Blend a few spoonfuls of the stock or water with the flour, then stir this mixture into the pan. Stir in the remaining stock or water and bring to a simmer, stirring. Add the bay leaves, Worcestershire sauce and tomato paste, then cover and cook gently for 1 hour, stirring occasionally. Uncover the pan toward the end of cooking to allow any excess water to evaporate, if necessary.

3 Preheat the oven to 375°F. Gently heat the potatoes for a couple of minutes, then mash with the butter, milk and seasoning. Add the tarragon and seasoning to the meat mixture and remove and discard the bay leaves, then pour the mixture into a pie dish.

4 Cover the meat with an even layer of potato and mark the top with the prongs of a fork. Bake for about 25 minutes, until golden brown. Serve garnished with a sprig of fresh tarragon.

Chicken, Leek and Parsley Pie

A creamy, herby chicken casserole encased in crispy pastry makes a delicious family meal.

Serves 4–6

INGREDIENTS
FOR THE PASTRY
2½ cups all-purpose flour
pinch of salt
⅞ cup butter, diced
2 egg yolks

FOR THE FILLING
3 chicken breasts
flavoring ingredients (bouquet
    garni, black peppercorns, onion
    and carrot)
4 tablespoons butter
2 leeks, thinly sliced
2 ounces Cheddar cheese, grated
1 ounce Parmesan cheese,
    finely grated
3 tablespoons chopped fresh parsley
2 tablespoons whole-grain mustard
1 teaspoon cornstarch
1¼ cups heavy cream
beaten egg, to glaze
salt and freshly ground black pepper
mixed green salad, to serve

Cheddar cheese
Parmesan cheese
leeks
butter
chicken breasts
parsley
all-purpose flour
cornstarch
whole-grain mustard
heavy cream
eggs

1 To make the pastry, first sift the flour and salt. Process the butter and egg yolks in a food processor or blender until creamy. Add the flour and process until the mixture is just coming together. Add about 1 tablespoon cold water and process for a few seconds more. Turn out onto a lightly floured surface and knead lightly. Wrap in plastic wrap and chill for about 1 hour.

2 Meanwhile, poach the chicken breasts in water to cover, with the flavoring ingredients added, until tender. Let cool in the liquid.

3 Preheat the oven to 400°F. Divide the pastry into two pieces, one slightly larger than the other. Roll out the large piece and use to line a 7 x 11-inch baking dish or pan. Prick the bottom with a fork and bake for 15 minutes. Let cool.

4 Lift the cooled chicken from the poaching liquid and discard the skin and bones. Cut the chicken flesh into strips, then set aside. Melt the butter in a frying pan and fry the leeks over low heat, stirring occasionally, until soft.

5 Stir in the Cheddar and Parmesan cheeses and chopped parsley. Spread half the leek mixture over the cooked pastry shell, leaving a border all the way around. Cover the leek mixture with the chicken strips, then top with the remaining leek mixture.

COOK'S TIP
This pastry is quite fragile and may break; the high fat content, however, means that you can patch it together by pressing pieces of pastry trimmings into any cracks that may appear.

6 Mix together the mustard, cornstarch and cream in a small bowl. Add salt and pepper to taste. Pour over the filling.

7 Moisten the edges of the cooked pastry shell. Roll out the remaining pastry and use to cover the pie. Brush with beaten egg and bake for 30–40 minutes, until golden and crisp. Serve hot, cut into square portions, with a green salad.

Chicken and Ham Pie

This domed double-crust pie is excellent for a cold buffet, picnics or any packed meals.

Serves 8

INGREDIENTS
14 ounces shortcrust pastry
1¾ pounds boneless chicken breasts
12 ounces uncooked ham
about 4 tablespoons heavy cream
6 scallions, finely chopped
1 tablespoon chopped
    fresh tarragon
2 teaspoons chopped fresh thyme
grated rind and juice of
    ½ large lemon
1 teaspoon freshly ground mace
beaten egg or milk, to glaze
salt and freshly ground black pepper

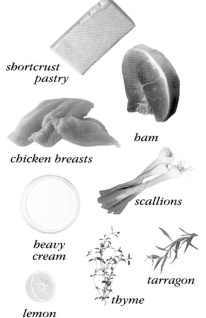

shortcrust pastry

ham

chicken breasts

scallions

heavy cream

tarragon

thyme

lemon

1 Preheat the oven to 375°F. Roll out one-third of the pastry and use it to line an 8-inch pie pan 2 inches deep. Place on a baking sheet.

2 Chop 4 ounces (one-seventh) of the chicken with the ham, then mix with the cream, scallions, herbs, lemon rind, 1 tablespoon of the lemon juice and the seasoning to make a soft mixture; add more cream if necessary.

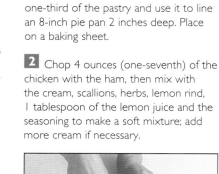

3 Cut the remaining chicken into ½-inch pieces and mix with the remaining lemon juice, the mace and salt and pepper.

COOK'S TIP
Make sure, when you are rolling out the pastry and lining the pie pan, that you don't stretch the pastry; otherwise it will shrink during cooking.

4 Make a layer of one-third of the ham mixture in the pastry shell, cover with half the chopped chicken, then add another layer of one-third of the ham. Add all the remaining chicken followed by the remaining ham mixture. Dampen the edges of the pastry shell. Roll out the remaining pastry to make a lid for the pie.

5 Use the trimmings to make a lattice decoration. Make a small hole in the center of the pie, brush the top with beaten egg or milk, then bake for about 20 minutes. Reduce the temperature to 325°F and bake for another 1–1¼ hours; cover the top with foil if the pastry becomes too brown. Transfer the pie to a wire rack and let cool.

Quiche Lorraine

The classic quiche is a delicious mixture of crumbly crust, custardy filling and smoky bacon flavor.

Serves 6

INGREDIENTS
12 ounces shortcrust pastry
8 ounces lean bacon strips, chopped
3 eggs
2 egg yolks
1½ cups whipping cream
½ cup milk
salt and freshly ground black pepper

shortcrust pastry

lean bacon

eggs

whipping cream

milk

VARIATIONS

Replace the bacon with diced cooked ham, and add 3 ounces grated Gruyère cheese.

For a vegetarian quiche, omit the bacon. Slice 1 pound zucchini and sauté in a little oil until lightly browned on both sides. Drain on paper towels, then arrange in the pastry shell. Sprinkle 2 ounces grated cheese on top. Make the egg mixture with 4 eggs, 1 cup cream, 4 tablespoons milk, ⅛ teaspoon grated nutmeg and salt and pepper.

1 Preheat the oven to 400°F. Roll out the pastry thinly and use to line a 9-inch pie pan. Prick the bottom of the pastry with a fork, then line with waxed paper and fill with baking beans. Bake "blind" for 15 minutes, then remove the paper and beans.

2 Cook the bacon in a frying pan until it is crisp and golden brown. Drain the bacon on paper towels.

3 Scatter the bacon in the partially baked pastry shell.

4 In a bowl, whisk together the eggs, egg yolks, cream and milk. Season with salt and pepper. Pour the egg mixture into the pastry shell.

5 Bake the quiche for 35–40 minutes, or until the filling is set and golden brown and the pastry is golden. Serve warm or at room temperature.

Beef and Stout Pie with Oysters

Layers of crisp puff pastry encase a tasty rich stew of tender beef and fresh oysters.

Serves 4

INGREDIENTS
1 pound stewing beef
2 tablespoons all-purpose flour
1 tablespoon sunflower oil
2 tablespoons butter
1 onion, sliced
⅔ cup Guinness stout
⅔ cup beef stock
1 teaspoon sugar
1 bouquet garni
12 oysters, opened
12 ounces puff pastry
1 egg, beaten
salt and freshly ground black pepper
chopped fresh parsley, to garnish

stewing beef

all-purpose flour

egg

beef stock

onion

stout

puff pastry

butter

sunflower oil

bouquet garni   oysters

1 Preheat the oven to 350°F. Trim any excess fat from the meat and cut into 1-inch pieces. Place the meat in a bag with the flour and plenty of seasoning. Shake until all the meat is well coated.

3 Pour the stout and stock into the casserole, then add the sugar and bouquet garni. Cover and cook in the oven for 1¼ hours.

4 Remove the casserole from the oven and discard the bouquet garni. Spoon the beef and the stout mixture into a large pie dish and set aside to cool for about 15 minutes. Increase the oven temperature to 400°F.

COOK'S TIP
The oysters are a delicious addition to this traditional Irish pie, but they are not essential. Omit them, if you prefer.

2 Heat the oil and butter in a flameproof casserole and sauté the meat for 10 minutes, until well sealed and browned all over. Add the sliced onion and continue cooking for 2–3 minutes, until just softened.

5 Meanwhile, remove the oysters from their shells and rinse. Dry on paper towels and stir into the beef and stout mixture.

6 Roll out the pastry to fit the pie dish. Brush the edge of the dish with the beaten egg and lay the pastry over the top. Trim neatly and decorate. Brush with the remaining egg and bake for 25 minutes, until puffed and golden. Serve immediately, garnished with parsley.

INDEX